CLOUDS
IN MY GUERNSEY
SKY

A memoir of love, truth and hope

Jag Sherbourne

**BLUE
ORMER**

Published by Blue Ormer Publishing.
www.blueormer.co.uk

Cover design and illustration by James Colmer.

Printed by Short Run Press, Exeter.

This is a true story. A small number of names and identifying characteristics have been changed to protect the privacy of those depicted.

ISBN 978-1-7396814-0-1

*For all the mothers in my family
and especially for Kathleen,
with whom it all began.*

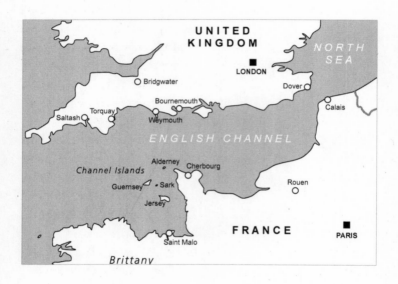

PART ONE

I have started this story over and over, never quite knowing from whose perspective to write it or how to steer it sensitively through the intersecting lives that have shaped it. This remarkable story happened to unremarkable people, the very people that I trusted most and who formed the bedrock of my world. They gifted me my happiness and spared me their pain, and I repaid them with the simple cruelty of taking them for granted. The familiarity of their touch, the intimacy of their smell, their idiosyncrasies and their love were the foods on which I flourished. Yet, when I look back, I sometimes wonder if I knew them at all.

When they passed they took with them the answers to all the questions that I never thought to ask, and left me with a childlike belief in the integrity of the life that we had shared together that survived unchallenged for at least half a century. I like to think my mother might have told me, had time not cheated her of the chance. My father did try to tell me, on occasion, but he never found a time when I was ready to listen. So I am left alone to piece together the jigsaw, with no picture for guidance, and with many pieces yet to be found.

Like all familiar journeys, the road I travelled forwards takes on a new perspective now I venture back. And, as I recreate their memories, I encounter the strangest irony of all, "La Raonde d'la Vie." "The circle of life." In truth, it is nothing more than Nature's carefully devised plan to divide us and rule, to keep the generations apart, promote the myth that children are somehow different from their parents, and mock us, when we eventually learn the truth, too late to set the records straight.

CHAPTER 1

Guernsey

CONVENTIONAL IS HOW I might have described my parents, Charles and Kathleen, as I was growing up, and naive is what they might reasonably have levelled at me, given that it was in everyone's best interests to appear conventional during the middle of the twentieth century. They raised me gently, with great sensitivity to my changing needs and an understated empathy that nurtured my well-being without ever seeking recognition or thanks. It is only now that I appreciate the selflessness of their care. As I was growing up l always wished for something different from them, some small eccentricity that might raise their credibility in my eyes, or more importantly in the eyes of my peers. But I never knew where to look and so found nothing.

Our home was the tiny island of Guernsey, a land so small that it fails to feature on most global maps, yet one that has been home to my family for generations. Guernsey lies a stone's throw from France and a giant's stride from the UK mainland, bathed by the cold and unpredictable waters of the English Channel and nestled on the fringes of the Bay of St Malo. It is the second-largest island of the archipelago known as the Channel Islands. Once part of the Duchy of Normandy and now a British Crown Dependency, Guernsey is too small to be fully independent, but we identify as Guernsey folk first, Channel Islanders second and British if we must.

As any resident will verify, you must be born and bred locally to be considered a true Guernsey "Donkey". I come from a long line of Donkeys, town dwellers mainly, each living just around the corner from the other, our lives mapped out in fairly predictable paths that didn't differ too much from the established norm. Or at least that is how it always seemed to me. Like all Donkeys we shared a stubborn loyalty to our roots, but it was my father who was most effusive in his passion for our island home. His love was unconditional, and he shared it with great pride whenever, and with whomever, the opportunity arose. Though he never had experience of living elsewhere, he firmly believed that he had struck lucky in life and it was infectious. My mother, on the other hand, kept her views so quietly to herself that I barely even noticed them. Perhaps she simply preferred to leave me to assume that she loved it too, which I was happy to do. Her perspective on our insular way of life must undoubtedly have been influenced by the five years she spent in the UK as an evacuee during World War 2, and would fascinate me now. But as I was growing up she seldom mentioned it and I never thought to ask.

Our family home lay right in the centre of the old town of St Peter Port. A charming neighbourhood of cobbled streets, narrow alleyways and randomly carved out flights of steps that cascaded down the hillsides all around us. Meandering and intertwined they created a gloriously haphazard, yet timeless beauty that is still in evidence today. But I was much too preoccupied with the business of growing up to concern myself with the nature of my surroundings, however interesting or exceptional they might have been.

In summer, like many Guernsey families, we spent most of our spare time on the beach. The island's beaches are as beautiful as any in the world and mostly more beautiful. From the rugged south coast cliffs that hide tiny horseshoe coves, to the vast stretches of sand on its more exposed west coast, Guernsey paints spectacular scenery on a variety of canvasses and all within easy reach. I was brought up on the beach and spent endless summer days with family and friends enjoying a freedom that was truly free. I still find it hard to imagine what people do in the summer if they have no beach they can go to; they probably wonder what I get up to in the winter.

The sweet-tempered breeze that cools us in summer is prone to turning moody and temperamental in winter. Gales whip the sea to a frenzy as it advances and retreats in defiant displays of beauty and rage. Occasionally, the ships stop sailing, the planes are grounded and we become cut off from the rest of the world. And mostly we just shrug our shoulders, hunker down and wait for it to pass, because that is how it is to live on an island. Our boundary is the ocean and we live, work and play, all sixty-three thousand of us, on the same twenty-four square miles of land. A land that delights and frustrates us, but not in equal measure.

The temperate climate and the more relaxed pace of life, combined with a natural resistance to change, are the seductive keepers of a traditional way of life in the Channel Islands. Despite this, Guernsey today basks in the international spotlight as a modern finance centre, with a thriving business community. It wasn't always like this. In the mid-twentieth century the main industries were fishing, horticulture and tourism. As a "townie" I had limited knowledge of the first two, but my mother ran a guest house during the summer months so I had considerable experience of the latter.

A multitude of "Bed and Breakfast" style establishments sprang up all over the island in the late 1940s as Guernsey became an increasingly popular holiday destination for UK tourists. There were few hotels in that early post-war era, and jobs were scarce, particularly for women, so the opening up of their homes to paid visitors gave an easy way for them to earn a little extra cash. Our B&B's offer was a comfortable bed for the night and morning tea, brought on a tray to the bedroom, followed by a hearty cooked breakfast each morning and an evening meal on Sundays. It involved sharing our family's basic facilities and meant that I was often restricted to playing in the kitchen or the backyard. Mum's hospitality was legendary and ensured that our home was generally full during the summer months, with many "regulars" who returned each year.

Guernsey still attracts visitors today but, with cheaper holiday deals and guaranteed sunshine available elsewhere, the island has needed to adapt what it has to offer. The personal touch of the B&Bs has long been replaced by the more polished provision of the new hotels. Rooms come with their own en-suites, televisions and tea and coffee-making facilities. Why share if you don't have to? And people come today, not just for the cultural experience, but to find out more about a history that the island has finally learnt to embrace and market as its selling point. Its occupation by Nazi Germany during World War 2.

The Channel Islands were the only British Territories to be occupied by the Germans during World War 2 and they remain, to this day, brimming with lives and a culture deeply affected by those dark times. Many islanders meander through their twenty-first-century lives unaware of the legacy of pain and suffering that underpins it; it was like that for me until a short while ago. Littered across our island lie concrete towers, camouflaged bunkers and anti-tank seawalls, all built during World War 2 to form part of Hitler's Atlantic Wall. These bastions of oppression, left in perpetuity as a reminder of our heritage, were all just part of my ordinary everyday. I barely even noticed them.

I walk the walks alone now, just one where once there were three, distracted by thoughts that disappear the moment I turn towards them. The passing of the years has brought a new kind of truth. Strange and unfathomable, it lingers on the sidelines, tantalisingly out of reach, as I try my best to catch it. But no one wins a game of hide and seek if they don't know how to look. My quest for answers drives me backwards, retracing my steps with caution and compassion, relearning our past and rewriting it as I go. And I do it, not just for the sake of my mother, who lived most of her life under the weight of its burden, but for the sake of all the women with similar stories who have been forced to bury them deep in the moral simplicities of the past.

I write this then for Kathleen; a happy woman with a sad story. My mother, and how she became my friend.

CHAPTER 2

Kathleen

WHEN I THINK OF my mother I remember most vividly the power of her humour and the infectious, beguiling laugh that brought its daily backdrop of cheer into our home. Laughter was her medicine and she partook of it freely, weaving her sense of fun into everything she did. She would chuckle gently with us whenever we slipped up, and more heartily when the mistake was her own. But it was at night, watching British comedy on the telly, when she really came alive. Her laughter drew us in and ensnared us, urging us to laugh with her at the misfortunes of the underdog and the absurdities of our everyday lives.

Mum was short and wholesome with a pleasant face and a ready smile. The kind of woman who is always on a diet but never seems to lose any weight. From an early age I towered above her, having got my height from my father, and my delight at this infuriated her.

"You can mock me all you like," she would protest, "but you'll be sorry when I'm gone!"

When she was two she won second prize in a national beauty contest, or at least her photo did, and, by all accounts, she was a real "looker" growing up. By the time I arrived on the scene, however, she was nearly forty and the years had taken their toll. Her thick, blonde hair had been coarsened by years of dubious treatments in the popular home salons of the times, and decades of Guernsey summers had etched a roadmap of intersecting lines deep into her face. She was still attractive, though, and even in the middle of winter her complexion never looked pale and sallow like mine or my father's. I always envied her that. It meant that all colours suited her, though she was too superstitious to ever wear green. Like many women of exceptional beauty she quietly and privately mourned its passing and could sometimes be caught smiling ruefully at her reflection, as if she were conspiring with her past to remember the power of its former glory.

Mum had brains, too, and was well-educated, having gained a scholarship to the local grant-aided Ladies College at eleven, and this secured her a good job at Boots the Chemist when she left school. So perhaps, in later life, her role as homemaker left her unfulfilled? She would never have admitted it though, preferring, outwardly at least, to enjoy what she had rather than dwell on what might have been. She favoured well-tailored clothes and expensive cosmetics which my father would buy her for special occasions, but other than that she was a woman not prone to extravagance. She loved routine, an orderly house and crosswords, and there was always a home-cooked meal on the table for us each evening or at lunchtime on a Sunday. She was a good mother to me, always very loving and kind, but she was never a soft touch; she left that to my father.

Mum's mum passed away well before I was born but her dad I knew quite well. Known as Pop Loveridge to just about everyone in the neighbourhood, he was a big man with bushy eyebrows, a hearty laugh and a thick Guernsey accent. He had a son and three daughters of which Mum was the oldest, Peg was the middle sister and Dink (named after her passion for Dinkie biscuits) was the youngest. Auntie Dink was taller than Mum and seemed to me much more elegant. She exuded a haughty stylishness that stemmed from her job as a fashion buyer for a local department store and I thought her impossibly glamorous. She lived just around the corner from us as I was growing up, with my Uncle George and their three children. I was particularly close to her only daughter, Val, who spent most of her free time at our house.

Mum's primary duty was always to feed us. There was a small convenience store nearby which delivered our basics each week but, for fresh food, we needed to go to the market. Twice a week she would march me through the faded, post-war neighbourhood, past windows dressed with gaudy ornaments and nicotine-stained curtains, until we reached the very centre of town.

First stop was always the fishmonger. Dressed in white overalls, stained by his bloodied task, we would find him standing to attention behind his stall, amiably immune to the desperate plight of the creatures that lay on their icy graves before him.

"Good morning Mrs Le Bargy!" he would say with a smile, "and what can I do for you today?"

"Depends what you have that's nice and fresh Mr Langlois. Maybe some nice fillets of plaice?"

And I would hide behind her coat, as the fish fixed their unblinking eyes straight on me and the stench of death caught in my throat. It was a relief when Mum had finally secured her purchase and could be tugged towards the lower halls of the market where the stalls piled high with fruit, vegetables and flowers stood. Intoxicated by the mêlées of colours and perfumes we would join the small queue that had gathered around the greengrocer. After a smile and a nod to each customer in turn, he would survey his produce with mock concentration, as if to affirm he would pick only the best to pop into the bag on his shiny steel scales. "Some lovely Victoria plums just for you Mrs Le Bargy. I know they're your favourite!"

Once our baskets were full we would make our way to Maison Carré, our reward for all the hours we had spent bargaining and queuing. Mum would pause in front of the shop window and I would press my face hard against the cold glass and wait whilst she marvelled at the sight of all the "fancies" on display.

"Look at those," she would whisper to herself before turning her attention to me.

"You are a lucky girl, Jackie. They never saw a cake here for five years during the Occupation you know. You are a very lucky girl indeed."

The repetition, designed to pin the sentiment to me, always fell wide of its mark. I was lucky in more ways than one, but it would take at least another half-century for me to truly comprehend the scale of my luck.

We are passing through the heavy glass doors and into the hot, sticky sweetness of the cake shop, the intoxicating smell of the pastries, and the garish colours of the icing and creams, have become the easy seducers of our post-war generation, and the queue at the counter is long and boisterous. In time we will join it, for the cakes are far too exquisite for us to leave empty-handed, but for the moment it is the upper salon that beckons us.

Sometimes we take the lift, but today we are too impatient to queue. My mother takes me by the hand so that we can climb the stairs together. They are dark and steep, and they make me feel nervous. Halfway up I pull hard on her arm, demanding that we stop to rest our legs and catch our breath; the 1960s tearoom above us is already in full swing. The rattle of bone china accompanies the rise and fall of chatter, each as jovial as the other, the same today as it was yesterday and will be tomorrow. Every so often we hear a wave of laughter rise up to the rafters and sweep around the room; a gift from woman to woman; the soundtrack to their lives.

At the top of the steps, my mother sweeps me up into her arms. The softness of her skin is my first ever memory, lightly scented with Coty L'Aimant, the perfume that my father gives her each Christmas. She seats me beside her and cuts into my cake, preordered by Auntie Dink and Val who have arrived before us. The flaky pastry, hardened by the pink icing, buckles at last under the insistence of her knife, custard oozing out of the sides of the layers sends saliva flooding into my mouth. Sugar, cream, and pastry convene for my pleasure and I gorge on the feast.

A girl sweeps upon us unexpectedly, urging us to widen our circle as she draws up a chair and sits herself down next to me. There is plenty of tea in the pot, but the cakes are all gone. She is full of smiles and tales to tell Val; they are about the same age. I have to work hard to distract her and claim her attention. Finally, she reaches towards me, kissing my head and tickling my ribs. As she withdraws to her own space she takes with her a piece of my cake.

"You are a lucky girl, Jack," she tells me. "A very lucky girl indeed."

CHAPTER 3

Charles

MY FATHER WAS MY first love. There's nothing unusual in that, but I was an only child and he was a shift worker so, with plenty of time to spend together during the days, the bond between us was especially strong. In time I would long for a brother or a sister to share in my childhood, but in the early years my father was my everything and I, in turn, was his shadow. I followed his every move, hung on his every word and clung to his every moment.

"Wait for me! I'm coming too!" I would cry, hurrying into my overalls whenever I saw him about to descend into the basement to tackle the miscellany of odd jobs that lay beneath us. The distinctive musty aroma that greeted us as we made our way cautiously down the steep, narrow steps is still my favourite smell; the smell of spending time with my father in our own secret space. And, when he finally sank into his armchair of an evening, I would fling a book at him and demand, "This one, Daddy! This one!" as I climbed onto his lap. "And please don't stop halfway. I want you to read it all!"

Even when he went to the bathroom I would sit on the step outside and wait for however long it took. Whilst many fathers might have considered such obsession an irritant, mine considered it a privilege. The only thing that could prise me away from him was his work, which took far too much of his time for my liking. But I knew I could wait all day for him to finish his shift, secure in the knowledge that he had waited his whole life for me and would never be too tired to play.

Dad was tall and lean, with a moustache and unruly black hair that he mostly succeeded in taming and polishing with Brylcreem. He had happy features and a slightly mischievous smile that always stood ready to break into an infectious laugh. But Dad was much more than handsome. Known by many as Charlie and by some as Charles, he was considered a man of integrity, maddeningly stubborn at times, but one who could be depended upon to treat everyone fairly and with compassion.

The eldest of five children, Dad was born in April 1915, three months before his parents married; he had made it into legitimacy, but only just. A sister and a brother arrived in quick succession, before his father, Albert, joined the Royal Guernsey Light Infantry and went off to serve in France for the last few months of World War 1. On his return to Guernsey, Albert fathered two more children and, by the late 1920s, the Le Bargy family was complete and living in a small terraced house in the centre of St. Peter Port. But times were hard. The family had little money and within a decade Dad had lost two of his siblings to natural causes and his father to alcohol. Nevertheless, his disposition remained one of contentment with life. When asthma confined him to bed on the day of his eleven plus, thereby stealing his chance of a secondary school education, he left school at fourteen without complaint and went, instead, to work at the local power station where he was to remain for the next five decades. Had his parents been better connected there would likely have been an appeal, because my father was undoubtedly clever, but with no one to fight his corner he was left to make up for this loss of education later in life with the help of correspondence school.

Our family home lay at the top of a steep hill known as Bosq Lane and, on a summer evening, Dad liked nothing better than to walk down to the bottom of the hill and take a stroll along the "Front", a stretch of coast road that runs along the east coast from St Sampsons in the north of the island to the main harbour further south. As soon as I could walk he took me with him. We would set off together, hand in hand, whilst I skipped and danced around him, bringing a smile to everyone we passed.

"Hello, Mr Le Bargy. Lovely evening isn't it? Goodness, how Jackie is growing! "

"Yes, indeed. We're off to see what's going on at the harbour," Dad would reply, his heart full of pride at this most simple of pleasures. The harbour was our magical place.

His brown slender fingers tighten around my tiny white ones signalling me to hurry across the busy main road; my life held securely in the palm of his hand.

As we reach the harbour the smells of oil and ocean curl around us like a blanket, filling our lungs with an intoxicating cocktail of salt and diesel. We deviate from the main walkway to stroll along the first pier, aware of the cranes working tirelessly overhead, swinging their heavy loads onto the boat moored beside the quay. But our eyes remain fixed on the ground beneath us as we take care not to stumble on the uneven surface. Before long we arrive at a flight of steps, a dark slippery pathway into the depths of the sea.

"Can we go down today Daddy?" I tug at his sleeve, begging him to take me. The malevolent shadows in the underground jetties entice me despite my fear.

"Not today sweetheart."

"Why not?" I pester, relieved yet still indignant.

"I have a bone in my leg!" he replies. It is always his excuse.

"Pigeons!" I scream, distracted by my favourite sight. Breaking free from his grip I run towards the crates piled high on the side of

the quay. The caged birds greet me with squawks and squabbles, spitting out fragments of feathers and sawdust that saturate the air all around us. Soon I am sneezing so hard that I cannot stop. Dad pulls out an old white hankie from his pocket, softened by a thousand washes, to soothe my discomfort as he gently steers me away from the birds.

"Let's leave them now darling. The cranes will be coming soon, to lift them onto the boat."

"And where will the boat take them, Daddy?" I ask him, as I always do, just to be sure.

And, as he answers, I let my imagination take flight to that far away place where the doors will be opened and the birds released, to make their long journey home. Pop is a pigeon fancier so I am well accustomed to the concept.

There is a chill in the air as we turn to walk back, hand in hand but quieter now, saving our energy for the final push up the hill. He will win of course, but it has to be fair. We pause at the bottom to catch our breath. As I grow stronger I will steal his energy, and the advantage he gives me will gradually fade to nothing, but I will make sure never to race against him unless I am certain he will win.

Mum is sitting on the wall at the top waiting to welcome us home and declare Dad the winner. She opens her arms to me and I fall into them as she lifts me up to sit beside her. A girl runs out of the house and launches herself at Dad as he struggles to regain his breath. She throws her arms around his neck, catching us all in the moment.

"Dinner's ready!" Mum says, breaking the spell, "wash your hands everyone and come to the table."

CHAPTER 4

Mum and Dad

MY PARENTS MARRIED IN 1938 and each year, on April 20th, they would celebrate the passing of time, not with flowers or chocolates, but quietly in their hearts. There was little talk of their wedding when I was growing up, and I have only one photograph of their special day, but they left behind an album full of pictures of their honeymoon in Cornwall of which they spoke often and proudly.

On their return to Guernsey, the newlyweds rented a house on the outskirts of St Peter Port within easy walking or cycling distance of their respective work, families and busy social life that centred around Town. Young people made their own entertainment in those days, gathering in each others' houses in winter or on the beach in summer. On special occasions, they held house parties, went roller-skating or stepped out onto a dance floor in one of the many ballrooms that lay scattered around the island. Theirs was a generation that would dress to impress; their lives the epitome of the nostalgic glamour that characterised the era.

Cinemas were popular, too, and my parents went to "the flicks" at least once a week. The dimly lit auditoriums could never quite shake off the rancid smell of stale smoke but were nonetheless generally full. As the first few bars of the National Anthem raised the audience to their feet, the thick velvet curtains would heave apart to reveal the magnificence of the big screen. And, as they sank back into their seats and the cigarettes lit up, the latest newsreel would play through the smoke, a precursor to the much anticipated main film.

These things I know for certain because my parents often reminisced about their courtship and the early years of their marriage. I know that they enjoyed a whole box of chocolates each time they went to the cinema, that they travelled first class to the UK for their honeymoon and that the house they first rented was brand new and in a smart neighbourhood of town. However, I never fully appreciated the wisdom of these early investments in their relationship, especially for a couple of such modest means.

Children seldom look beyond the ordinary to see the extraordinary in the lives of their parents, and I was no exception. To me, each disparate event that they chose to share with me existed purely in its own cameo moment in time, untouched by the ebb and flow of other events playing out all around them. I trusted them to tell me what I needed to know with no thought for what might lie beneath the superficiality of the stories. Yet it was their emotional journey that was most significant in shaping the people they were to become. And of that, they never spoke.

It was only with the passing of time that I finally managed to close the gap on our generational divide. Firstly, as I embarked upon the tricky road of parenthood myself and suddenly understood the hurt that my mother, in particular, must have felt at all my thoughtlessness. And secondly, when her story finally found its wings, and I found myself compelled to follow it, back through the decades, to the start of her life with my father.

I became the archaeologist of their past, meticulously scraping away the burial layers to uncover tiny fragments of their lives that lay scattered along the way. Fragments that, when pieced together, added up to a story quite different to the one I remembered growing up. An intriguing story of lives more interesting than I could ever have imagined; lives I knew nothing about. And as the events, good and bad, began to attach themselves to their timeline, the search for the woman that my mother had been, and the man who had always supported her, began to take on a whole new meaning.

CHAPTER 5

Evacuation

A YEAR INTO THEIR marriage Mum and Dad found themselves expecting their first child; they were delighted. Though life in Guernsey was plodding along as usual, all around them the global stage was changing. The Treaty of Versailles had failed to subjugate the Teutonic resolve and Germany's covert plans for rearmament were beginning to reach fruition; a world war lay on the horizon. When Germany invaded Poland on 1st September 1939 the allies finally decided to act, but by this time Hitler's war machine was unstoppable.

My mother was five months pregnant, and enjoying a day on the beach with my father, when they heard the news that Britain and France had declared war on Germany. It was hard to imagine conflict in the benevolent warmth of that early September sun, and they felt no immediate need for concern. The message to the British people was that the war would be over quickly and, in any case, Guernsey could rely on the UK government to defend it. Or so it believed.

Throughout the ensuing winter, the signs remained promising. The war seemed to have stopped before it had properly started and the lack of action during the "Phoney War", as those first few months were later to be known, lulled the Allies into a false sense of security.

Meanwhile, in Guernsey, Mum's pregnancy was progressing well. On 31st January 1940, at the Lady Ozanne Nursing Home in St Peter Port, she gave birth to a baby boy and named him Michael John. But my parent's happiness was short-lived. Just six weeks later, on 13th March 1940, the colours of their hope turned to grey in their despair as they watched Michael pass away following what would today be considered routine bowel surgery. My father, a moderate man in so many respects, lived the rest of his life with a strong aversion to the number 13. It never crossed my mind to ask him why.

To help deal with their loss they moved house immediately, back into the heart of Town, to the streets they had known as children, to live beside the people that they loved. Supposedly named after Rome, but with a 1940s-style "typo," they rented a house called "Romo". It was a commonplace, mid-terrace town-house with a small back yard and an even tinier front garden that was home to the most spectacular fuchsia bush in the entire neighbourhood. The crimson flowers, with their pearly white petticoats, charmed many a passer-by, grateful for a reason to stop and catch their breath at the top of the steep hill known as Bosq Lane. Romo stood on three floors and boasted four bedrooms, two good-sized reception rooms, a well-equipped kitchen and a large underground basement complete with a coal hole.

As my parents settled into their new home, the war across Europe started to pick up pace. By the end of May France was falling and the British, outmanoeuvred onto the beaches of Dunkirk, were finding themselves increasingly isolated.

In the Channel Islands, the mood had darkened. Mum and Dad's new life, in the centre of town, had placed them right at the epicentre of the fear and chaos that was threatening to overwhelm the island. Each night the sound of gunfire from the near continent, a little over 30 miles away, was faintly audible from their attic bedroom. By day, however, holidaymakers were still walking the streets of St Peter Port, and this normality made it hard to imagine that the Germans, despite all the news reports of their rapid advances through Europe, could possibly pose a threat to the tiny communities in the Channel Islands.

By mid-June explosions could clearly be heard from across the water and boatloads of French refugees started arriving in St Peter Port harbour. Reports of a small German reconnaissance aircraft flying low over the island spread panic and fear that the Germans were about to invade. Yet the hedgerows were their usual riot of colour and the unfettered joy of the birds in the morning gave the superficial reassurance that all was still well, even as many of their friends and neighbours started to leave the island for the perceived safety of the UK mainland.

With news of the German occupation of the Cherbourg peninsula came the promise of a place on an evacuation boat for any islander who wished to leave for the mainland. A rumour that evacuation was compulsory began to circulate before quickly being squashed by the authorities.

Indecision and panic swept across the island. Should people stay or should they leave was the question at every dinner table, in every pub and on every street corner. No one had the slightest idea what to do for the best.

On the 18th June, all public places of entertainment including cinemas, theatres and dance halls closed their doors, as did all of the primary schools. The next day the Bailiff and acting Lieutenant Governor of Guernsey, Victor Carey, issued the following statement, reported on the front page of The Star newspaper:

ISLAND EVACUATION
ALL CHILDREN TO BE SENT TO MAINLAND TOMORROW
Mothers May Accompany Those Under School Age
REGISTRATION TONIGHT
WHOLE BAILIWICK TO BE DEMILITARISED
Strong Advice To Men Between 20 and 33

For islanders, who had come to depend on the benevolence of the Great British Empire, the prospect of being left alone and defenceless was terrifying. The British Government had decided that the Channel Islands held no strategic value to either side in the conflict, but would Hitler agree? The recommendation that schoolchildren should leave the island immediately suggested not.

Parents were instructed to register their children by 7pm that evening if they wished them to leave the island. They would evacuate, with their schools, and be accompanied by their teachers. Only mothers with infants would be permitted to travel with their children. Each child was to bring one small suitcase of essentials which should include warm clothes for the winter.[1] Families had just a few hours to reach their decision. Guernsey did not sleep at all that night.

Those who chose evacuation for their children took them to their school in the early hours of the following morning and delivered them into the care of their teachers at the school gate. Public shows of emotion were discouraged and the goodbyes were deliberately kept brief. The authorities had hoped to keep the distress of the public well away from the harbour as the boats were departing, but for some parents the agony of separation proved unbearable. Fearing they had made a terrible

---

1   See Exhibit A.

mistake, they made their way straight down to the harbour to claim their children back as they arrived at the quayside, a few even snatched them away from their school party as they began to board the boats.

The Press Diary reported the simple observation that …

mass hysteria was noticeable.

There were further reports of one evacuee selling his new high-powered car on the quay for just one pound, of farmers arriving at the boat having slaughtered all their cattle rather than leaving them to starve, and of publicans giving out free drinks and selling their cigarettes at one shilling per packet to clear their stocks. For everyone, such a rapid departure was accompanied by significant personal sacrifice. There was pain and anguish, indecision and fear, as the islanders of Guernsey were forced to face up to the uncertainty of their future.

By mid-June nearly half the population had evacuated and it had become clear that there would not be room on the evacuation boats for everyone who wanted to leave. Towards the end of June, the Bailiff issued the following statement to those who remained:

Beyond teachers, children of school age and under with mothers or other relatives in charge, as well as men of military age it is impracticable for others to hope to be evacuated.

Meanwhile, my parents were in limbo. Dad had applied for National Service when war broke out and was still waiting to hear when, and in what capacity, he would be needed. The electricity board had promised to release him from his role as an essential worker at the power station when his call came. He and Mum had decided they would evacuate together as soon as he was given the go-ahead. But Pop had other ideas.

"Kathy love, I have two tickets for the boat that leaves the day after tomorrow. I want you to go and take Dinkie with you," he told her, "I reckon Lil and Bert will put you up if we drop them a line."

"I can't do that, Dad. I'm not going anywhere without Charles … we're still waiting to hear …"

"Think about it Kathy love," he interrupted. He was fond of his eldest daughter and convinced that what he was offering her was the best solution for everyone. "Who knows what the Germans are capable of? Dink is only 17, and you're at risk too. You've heard of the things they get up to. Charlie will get a ticket when his time comes, no trouble. They're practically forcing young men like him to go. As soon as he's released from work he'll be gone. But what about you, Kathy love? Charlie will be gone and there may not be any tickets left for the likes of you … if you leave it any later."

"Dad I just can't …"

"You can love. It's for the best. Talk to Charlie … I'm sure he'll agree with me."

How long it took my parents to reach their decision I can only imagine. Still raw with grief from the loss of their first-born it can't have been easy. But in the end, Mum did board that ship with her sister, trusting that Dad would follow at a later date. Had they decided differently I would have another story to tell, or perhaps no story at all.

The sisters departed in such haste that there was no time to confirm arrangements with Lil and Bert, so they had little choice but to call in a family favour. On arrival in Weymouth, they headed straight for their uncle's house in Saltash, Cornwall, in the hope that he might be able to help them temporarily.

As predicted, their stay with him was to prove short-lived. A couple of days later a letter arrived, bearing a Guernsey stamp and written in their mother's hurried hand.

Guernsey

28th June 1940

My Dear Kath and Dinkie,

Hope you are alright and that Uncle Harry could put you up. Had a wire from Lily, came too late for you, she will be only too pleased to put you up.

Things are quiet here. Am longing to hear from you.

Peg sends her love.

All my love,

Mummie xxx

Lily and her husband Bert were old family friends who lived in Bridgwater, Somerset, and this was good news for my mother who had always found them to be amenable and kind. But, as the sisters prepared to make their way to Bridgwater, word that the Germans had carried out terrible atrocities directly over their homes in Guernsey was already starting to make its way across the English Channel.

CHAPTER 6

Occupation

DAD WORKED AS AN engineer at the local power station. It was a job he would stay in for his entire working life and, though he changed to a managerial desk job well before he retired, in the early days he worked shifts. Aside from the variations in his shifts, Dad was in every other way a man of routine. Whenever he had a free evening during the summer he would wander down to the harbour.

The evening of Friday 28th June 1940 was still and warm and had all the potential to be perfect for such a stroll, but Dad had business to attend to first. On finishing his shift, he headed straight for Pop Loveridge's cottage at number 6 Upper Canichers, two streets up from the Front, to see if there was any news of Mum and Dink.

"The girls got to Harry's okay, but they'll be moving on to Bridgwater soon, to stay with Lil," Pop told him as they shared a drink and a cigarette together in the garden. "Lil said they can stay as long as they like. She'll look after them well, Charlie, don't you worry."

"That's great news!" Dad said, relieved that his wife and sister-in-law had arrived safely, and grateful that they had found somewhere more permanent to stay. Since Kath and Dink's departure he had been busy preparing, not just for his own evacuation, but also for that of his mother and youngest sister, Betty. He had been assured by the authorities that they would be given tickets to evacuate with him as soon as his necessary permissions came through. His other sister, Muriel, had decided that she would not evacuate with them.

"Well," Dad continued, about to stand up, "I'd best get back home to see how Mum and Betty are settling in. I've persuaded them to live with me at Romo … thought it best … just in case we're given the go ahead to evacuate at short notice. They moved in this morning."

Pop put out his hand to stop him. "Sit down Charlie and have another smoke. Your folks will be fine. It's a lovely evening and it's still early."

Smoking was a habit that would eventually claim Dad's life, long after he had given it up at my insistence. But on that particular evening, it was a second cigarette, at the persuasion of my grandfather, that actually saved his life.

They heard the planes before they saw them, the low hum of the unwelcome intruders on an otherwise idyllic evening. At 7pm the first bombs fell and the machine guns began to discharge their deadly rounds. Dad and Pop watched helplessly as the German planes, in waves of three, rained terror over the island for the next fifty minutes. But why were so many bombs being dropped on the harbour? And why on the very day when British military experts had declared "there need be no fear of the Germans taking any advantage from the British decision to demilitarise the Channel Islands"?

Unknown to them, the British Government had not yet informed the enemy that the Channel Islands had been demilitarised and it was the unfortunate tomato lorries, and their resemblance to military vehicles as they waited in line to offload their cargos, that bore the brunt of that oversight. Their drivers, together with the passers-by who had taken shelter under them, stood no chance in the raging infernos that ensued. Even the ambulance was targeted as it sped up St Julian's Avenue and, out at sea, the coxswain and his son were killed in the lifeboat. Guernsey was left in shock at the extent of such unprecedented atrocity. By the time the all-clear was sounded at around 8pm, thirty-three Guernsey men and women had lost their lives, dozens more had been injured and forty-nine vehicles lay burning along the Front. Warily, the islanders left the safety of their shelters, and shouted and screamed their way to finding out the fate of their missing loved ones.

As fear tightened its grip on the locals, many ran from their hiding places to board the last of the evacuation boats that had been about to leave the island when the bombing started. Others chose to sleep with friends or relatives outside of Town that night. My dad returned home as soon as he considered it safe to do so. As he ran the short distance along the Canichers, glass and debris from damaged houses littered the road but Romo stood, untouched, just a few metres up from the centre of the bombings. To his relief, Dad found his mum and sister, along with several of their neighbours, huddled together in the basement of the house, badly shaken but otherwise safe and well. The sirens proclaiming the all-clear gently coaxed them out of their hiding place, replacing fear with curiosity. They walked, together, to the bottom of Bosq Lane to view the devastation. Fires raged in the queue of tomato lorries lined up alongside the pavement and the old Weighbridge Clock Tower had been badly damaged. The clock had stopped at 7pm. It would be some time before the human cost of the raid would be discovered but the main fear of all the islanders had become what would happen next. They would not have to wait long to find out.

The news of the bombing reached England almost immediately with reports of many casualties, though the details were sketchy and there was no information as to who had been killed. My mother endured many dark hours trying to find out whether her family were alive or dead. Until, finally, the telegrams arrived in tandem, each the eerie echo of the other.

ALL SAFE. DON'T WORRY. CHARLES.

ALL SAFE. DON'T WORRY. MUMMIE AND DADDY.

The advancing war had set the seal on their separation and, as Mum and Dink stepped off the train and into the arms of their Bridgwater welcome, the Germans were already commencing the occupation of their homeland. As the sisters arrived at the end-of-terrace house in the centre of Bridgwater that was to become their home for the next five years, the jackboots were marching through the streets of St Peter Port. And, as they sat down to dinner with their host family, all lines of communication between Guernsey and the UK were severed. The unknown stretched ahead of them, and all hope of Dad joining Mum any time soon, had abruptly become a dream of the past.

CHAPTER 7

The War Years

WHEN A GERMAN RECONNAISSANCE aircraft landed in Guernsey on the morning of Sunday 30th June the pilot expected resistance but found, instead, that the airport was almost deserted. Later that day a platoon of German airmen was flown into the island and was met by a local policeman carrying a letter signed by the Bailiff.

> This island has been declared an Open Island by His Majesty's Government of the United Kingdom. There are no armed forces of any description. The bearer has been instructed to hand this communication to you. He does not understand the German language.

The most senior German officer was then taken straight to the Royal Hotel to meet the Bailiff and other local officials to inform them that the occupation of the island had begun. The Royal Hotel lay at the bottom of Bosq Lane, just a few metres down the hill from Romo.

The next day the front page of the Guernsey Press, read as follows:

ORDERS OF THE COMMANDANT OF THE GERMAN FORCES
ON THE OCCUPATION OF THE ISLAND OF GUERNSEY

1.   ALL INHABITANTS MUST BE INDOORS BY 11P.M. AND MUST NOT LEAVE THEIR HOMES UNTIL 6A.M.

2.   WE WILL RESPECT THE POPULATION IN GUERNSEY; BUT, SHOULD ANYONE ATTEMPT TO CAUSE THE LEAST SIGN OF TROUBLE, SERIOUS MEASURES WILL BE TAKEN AND THE TOWN WILL BE BOMBED.

3.   ALL ORDERS GIVEN BY THE MILITARY AUTHORITY ARE TO BE STRICTLY OBEYED.

4.   ALL SPIRITS ARE TO BE LOCKED UP IMMEDIATELY, AND NO SPIRITS MAY BE SUPPLIED OBTAINED OR CONSUMED HENCEFORTH. THIS PROHIBITION DOES NOT APPLY TO STOCKS IN PRIVATE HOUSES.

5.   NO PERSON SHALL ENTER THE AERODROME AT LA VILLIAZE.

6.   ALL RIFLES, AIRGUNS, PISTOLS, REVOLVERS, DAGGERS, SPORTING GUNS, AND ALL OTHER WEAPONS WHATSOEVER, EXCEPT SOUVENIRS, MUST, TOGETHER WITH ALL AMMUNITION, BE DELIVERED TO THE ROYAL HOTEL BY 12 NOON TODAY, JULY 1ST.

7.   ALL BRITISH SAILORS, AIRMEN AND SOLDIERS ON LEAVE ON THIS ISLAND MUST REPORT AT THE POLICE STATION AT 9A.M. TODAY, AND MUST THEN REPORT AT THE ROYAL HOTEL.

8.   NO BOAT OR VESSEL OF ANY DESCRIPTION, INCLUDING ANY FISHING BOAT, SHALL LEAVE THE HARBOUR OR ANY OTHER PLACE WHERE THE SAME IS MOORED, WITHOUT AN ORDER FROM THE MILITARY AUTHORITY, TO BE OBTAINED AT THE ROYAL HOTEL. ALL BOATS ARRIVING FROM JERSEY, FROM SARK OR FROM HERM, OR ELSEWHERE, MUST REMAIN IN HARBOUR UNTIL PERMITTED BY THE MILITARY TO LEAVE. THE CREW WILL REMAIN ON BOARD. THE MASTER WILL REPORT

TO THE HARBOUR MASTER, ST. PETER PORT, AND WILL OBEY HIS INSTRUCTIONS.

9. THE SALE OF MOTOR SPIRIT IS PROHIBITED, EXCEPT FOR USE ON ESSENTIAL SERVICES, SUCH AS DOCTOR'S VEHICLES, THE DELIVERY OF FOODSTUFFS, AND SANITARY SERVICES WHERE SUCH VEHICLES ARE IN POSSESSION OF A PERMIT FROM THE MILITARY AUTHORITIES TO OBTAIN SUPPLIES. THESE VEHICLES MUST BE BROUGHT TO THE ROYAL HOTEL BY 12 NOON TODAY TO RECEIVE THE NECESSARY PERMISSIONS. THE USE OF CARS FOR PRIVATE PURPOSES IS FORBIDDEN.

10. THE BLACKOUT REGULATIONS ALREADY IN FORCE MUST BE OBSERVED AS BEFORE.

11. BANKS AND SHOPS WILL BE OPEN AS USUAL.

(Signed) THE GERMAN COMMANDANT
OF THE ISLAND OF GUERNSEY
JULY 1ST, 1940

This was the first of a constantly evolving stream of orders that would be revised and extended by the enemy during its occupation. By the end of the first week, the island had adopted German time, was adapting to the introduction of the reichsmark and had introduced rationing on meat, butter, sugar, salt, tea, coffee and cocoa. In addition, there was robust encouragement for islanders to drink more milk and eat more tomatoes, both of which were in plentiful supply. It was in everyone's best interests to conserve vital supplies and, by the end of the summer, significant measures had been put in place to this effect.

As summer turned to autumn, the islanders gradually adapted to life under this new regime. Many of the schools reopened to cater for the one thousand or so children who remained on the island, whilst large consignments of food began to arrive from France. Life began to evolve into a new kind of normal and the mood of the islanders was given a further boost when a trickle of Red Cross letters began to arrive, delivering messages from loved ones who had evacuated.

It was not until the 4th March 1941 that my father received the small postcard from the Controlling Committee of the States of Guernsey with the news that he had been waiting for:

Dear Mr Le Bargy,

A communication for you has been received through the International Red Cross from Mrs K. A. Le Bargy.

If you call at Elizabeth College between 10.30am and 12.30pm on any morning, or between 2.30pm and 5pm on any afternoon (except Thursday), you can see the communication and send a reply not exceeding 25 words.

If you do not call within seven days of the above date, it will be concluded that you do not wish to send a reply.[2]

He went immediately to Elizabeth College to read his letter and to write his response. He was so eager to receive word from her that it was hard not to be disappointed …

23rd November 1940
Dearest Charles. Am safe. Well. All my love.

To make matters worse he was instructed to write his reply on the reverse of the letter which would then be returned to her. He would be left with no keepsake. So he copied her words

---

2   For details of the Red Cross Message Service, see Exhibit B.

onto the back of the postcard that he had been instructed to bring with him so that he might always remember them. Eight words when she should have been allowed twenty-five and scrawled in an untidy hand very unlike that of his wife's. There was no signature, no kisses, nothing at all of her. The letter had been sent from Bath so she must have relayed the message over the phone, and it had taken more than three months to reach him. At least now, though, he would be able to write to her. Islanders were only allowed to send a Red Cross message if they had received one first. He had thought carefully about how he might use each one of his twenty-five words to good effect. Only 'family news of strictly personal character' was allowed and he had no intention of jeopardising his precious first words.

4th March 1941
Dearest Kath, Received your card. Don't worry. All well. Am living in "Romo" with Mum and Betty. See your folk regularly. All my love, Charles

Soon islanders would be permitted to send one letter each month to loved ones in the UK, regardless of whether any had been previously received. Dad wrote to Mum every month, but his efforts did not always seem to be reciprocated ...

27th October 1941
Darling Kath, Anxious for news, received only one message dated November 1940. Have sent several messages c/o Mrs Finch. Everyone here O.K. Please reply. Charles

Sixteen months had passed since he had last seen his wife and, in that time, he had received just eight words from her. Meanwhile, life under enemy occupation felt increasingly uneasy. The Germans had started inflicting the harshest of punishments for any behaviour which they perceived as subversive. It would not be long before keeping pigeons became an offence that would carry the death penalty. As 1941 drew to a close all photography was banned, the entire south coast had been designated a prohibited zone, along with some stretches of the west coast, and identity cards had been issued to all islanders. The Christmas rations that year would allow each person an extra 1oz meat, 2oz sugar, 1 oz salt and 1½ oz tea. A grand total of 5½ oz of festive cheer.

As the war years rolled on, many islanders convicted of crimes were sent to internment camps in Europe. But, in spite of the ever-present danger, Dad never lost his sense of humour. He learnt to speak German so that he could converse with the young German soldiers. Sometimes, if he felt mischievous and was confident that he wouldn't be understood, he would smile broadly, nod his head vigorously and speak to a soldier in English.

"You really are a revoltingly, ugly piece of work aren't you? You fat pompous windbag."

And, much to his amusement, the German would smile back and nod his head equally enthusiastically, deliciously oblivious to Dad's insults. He never tried this trick at night, though, when he was called to "HALT" in the glare of a German searchlight on his way home from a late shift. Then, he would rely on his German vocabulary and his out-of-curfew pass to steer him safely out of danger.

Towards the end of the war, life became significantly more difficult for all the inhabitants of the Channel Islands, whichever side of the conflict they were on. After D-Day essential supply lines from Europe were severed and both the occupying forces and the civilian populations were effectively left to starve.

Scribbled at the foot of the UK cabinet meeting minutes of 27th September 1944, in Sir Winston Churchill's handwriting, was the following directive:

Let 'em starve. No fighting. They can rot at their leisure.

The Germans responded by closing down all the schools, theatres and playing fields and prepared to introduce a communal cooking and feeding programme. Essential rations had been reduced to almost nothing, and life had become especially difficult for the inhabitants of Romo. Living in town meant that they had no land on which they could grow their own food and they owed their survival to the kindness of family and friends and whatever they could scrounge from the black market.

As autumn turned to winter rations were further restricted and it was clear that the gas supply would shortly run out. In November the Bailiff was given permission from the German military authorities to send the following letter to the Secretary-General of the International Red Cross:

5th November 1944
Conditions rapidly deteriorating here. Will soon become impossible. We appreciate difficulties, but civilian population needs urgent supplies of essentials. We urge immediate visit of Red Cross representative. All rations drastically reduced.
Bread will last until 15th December. Fat production much below consumption. Soap and other cleansers – stocks completely exhausted. Vegetables generally inadequate. Salt stocks exhausted. Clothing and footwear – stocks almost exhausted. Coal stocks exhausted. Wood fuel quite inadequate. Many essential medical supplies already finished.

(Signed) Victor G. Carey, Bailiff of Guernsey

In reply, the International Red Cross Ship the SS Vega set sail from Lisbon on 20th December 1944 bound for the Channel Islands carrying food parcels donated by the citizens of Canada and New Zealand. The cargo also consisted of medical supplies, salt, soap, a small quantity of clothing for small children and 96,000 cigarettes. It arrived in Guernsey on December 27th and returned every month with its life-saving cargos, until the end of the war. Many islanders would not have survived the final months of the war without this humanitarian effort and the visits of the aid ship were always times of great excitement and celebration. The Germans, too, were close to starvation, yet they permitted the aid ships access to the harbour and ensured that their precious cargo did, generally, reach its intended recipients. Any German caught trying to steal from the parcels was dealt with severely, but it was not unusual to find them at night, roaming the streets and searching through dustbins for tiny discarded scraps.

The arrival of spring in 1945 brought hope that the war was finally coming to an end, but it wasn't until 3pm on Tuesday 8th May that Winston Churchill verified that all German land, sea and air forces had surrendered.

Hostilities will end officially at one minute after midnight tonight, but in the interests of saving lives the "cease fire" began yesterday to be sounded all along the front, and our dear Channel Islands are also to be freed to-day.

Churchill's words held little sway with the occupying forces of the Channel Islands however, who were determined to hold on to their slice of British territory for as long as possible. As HMS Bulldog and HMS Beagle set sail from Plymouth, charged with accepting the surrender, the German authorities issued a warning that they would be fired upon by shore batteries should they come too close to the island. The ceasefire was not scheduled to come into operation until after midnight and the Channel Islands would be obliged to wait one more day to be officially liberated.

As dawn broke on Wednesday 9th May 1945, the grey outline of the two Royal Navy ships, lying at anchor just outside of the harbour, came into focus. People from all over the island had descended upon St Peter Port and were already lining the quay. By 7am the relevant paperwork had been signed and, at 8am, the first of the landing parties pulled up alongside the jetty. The vast crowds that had gathered shouted and wept as the Tommies started to make their way through them towards the centre of town. Men shook their hands to congratulate them, women hugged them a little too tightly and everyone made a grab for the sweets, oranges and other small treats and trinkets that were thrown their way. Soldiers and civilians alike were reduced to tears by the enormity of the moment.

Town had never seen such crowds and, as Dad stood amongst them, his tendency towards moderation was momentarily trumped by the extraordinary displays of emotion all around him. After the troops had passed, he made his way through the sea of people to a friend's apartment in the High Street to celebrate the rest of the day with family and friends.

Soon islanders would be able to reach out, beyond the 25 censored words they had been permitted to send each month, to loved ones from whom they had been separated for the five long years of the war. What messages would this new freedom of speech carry and how would they be received by those whose own experience of war had been viewed from a very different perspective? My father, determined to enjoy every minute of that first Liberation Day, had few concerns regarding contacting his wife. He had heard very little from her during their separation but his spirit remained undeterred. His first letter was already written. It sat on the ledge in the entrance porch at Romo waiting to be sent as soon as he was able to purchase a stamp:

Romo
Bosq Lane,
V Day, 8th May 1945

Darling Kath,

At last the day has come, you can have no concept as to how we in Guernsey feel today after five years under German rule. The people here are in high spirits though there is not much outward sign of jubilation, as we feel that our day of real celebrations is yet to come.

The majority of the population have little food to have even as a celebration tea. Hundreds of families having only bread and that rationed, and no butter to put on it, not only for tea, but in the majority of cases for dinner also. However the Red Cross ship left here yesterday and tomorrow we get a parcel, and believe me we are going to tuck in.

Since Christmas we have had only small quantities of potatoes and all other vegetables, and indeed in the last two months these have failed almost entirely, so that we've been living almost entirely on Red Cross supplies i.e. one parcel in three weeks and 5lbs bread per person per week.

Cigarettes are at a premium and darling if you knew what I had to pay today for eight cigarettes to celebrate V day well I don't know what you'd say, anyway I'll tell you nine reichsmarks per cigarette! That is £7 - 13s - 0d for eight!

We haven't even a drink. I could write for hours and tell you things that you could hardly believe, however I shall wait till we meet. In the meantime darling here's hoping for a speedy reunion, and if you get the chance please send me some smokes.

I am fit and well and have not altered much, the older people seeming to be affected by the lack of food more than us young uns.

Well this is short and sweet so I'll say cheerio for now,

love to Dinks and Junior,

All my love, Charles XXXXXXX

PS Excuse pencil ink is very scarce

CHAPTER 8

The Return

WHILST THE LAST SCENES of World War 2 were playing out on the global stage, the writing of the script for the new post-war era was well underway. As the world struggled to determine what peace should look like, the impending liberation of the Channel Islands posed a unique challenge, not only logistically, but also in its social complexity. The evacuation had taken a little over a week in June 1940 but it had long been predicted that the repatriation of the evacuees would be a far lengthier and even more emotive process.

Channel Island Societies had formed across the UK during the war, to offer support for the evacuees, to give news of their fellow islanders on the mainland, and information on what had been happening back home. The most prominent of these societies was the Stockport and District Channel Island Society which had started publishing "The Channel Islands Monthly Review Journal of Channel Island Refugees in Great Britain" in June 1941.

The June 1944 journal issued the following warning:

For a considerable time no one will be able to go to the islands whose services there are not urgently required for work connected with the war efforts, and only in the most exceptional cases will anyone be allowed to leave the Islands.[3]

---

3   See Exhibit C.

As the machinations of war ground inexorably to a halt many evacuees, including those who had longed for home and a reunion with loved ones, found themselves facing the prospect of return with more than a little trepidation. As the days of their evacuation had turned into weeks, months and eventually years, they had seized the opportunity to play out their lives on a much larger stage than that of the tiny island home that had raised them. Most had fashioned new and fulfilling roles for themselves and the women, in particular, were enjoying the new sense of purpose and financial independence that their wartime work had provided.

The five years apart had also given everyone ample time to reflect on the circumstances surrounding their evacuation. Some had been called cowards, others deserters, and even as they had boarded the ships to take them away there had been signs on the quay urging them to stay.

KEEP YOUR HEADS!
DON'T BE YELLOW!
BUSINESS AS USUAL

Now, the hurt that these messages had caused the evacuees five years ago was turning to anxiety as they wondered what sort of reception they might expect on their return.

In April 1945 the Central Advisory Committee for Channel Island Affairs was set up to consider how the return of the evacuees might be managed. During the inaugural meeting, the committee recognised not only the concerns of the returning evacuees but also the circumstances of their kinsmen that had remained.

Five years of separation and widely different living conditions cannot fail to give each of the two groups a different outlook; nor is this the only difficulty, for the stress and strain of the Occupation is said to have brought about differences among those who remained, two of the principal causes being the attitude adopted towards the Occupying Power and the Black Market.

Thus it may be anticipated that at least three groups will be concerned in building the future for the prosperity and happiness of the Islands. Unless a large measure of 'give and take' can be achieved among all islanders, and unless each group can bring itself to allow that the others also have a point of view, and unless all are prepared to find common ground for their mutual benefit, rehabilitation may be a bitter and prolonged process. [4]

By June 1945 the Channel Islands Refugees Committee had started to issue practical advice as to what the evacuees needed to do and what they might reasonably expect.

The immediate return to the islands of large numbers of persons would create very serious problems of accommodation and unemployment, and at the outset provision can be made for the return of only a few hundred persons per week. Later the rate will increase as employment and accommodation become available.

The island authorities will be responsible for allotting priorities, and persons who will be selected for early return will be Channel Islanders for whom there is immediate employment in the islands and those who have homes to go to and for whom reabsorption would not create local problems.

All residents of Jersey, Guernsey, or Sark wishing to return should apply by post and not in person, to the passport office, Channel

4   See Exhibit D.

Islands section, Dartmouth Street, London, S.W.1, for the forms of application. They will be told how to proceed and will be notified when their return to the Channel Islands has been authorised. It is particularly requested that an application for return to the islands should not be made unless the applicant is prepared to travel at short notice.[5]

Whatever Mum felt emotionally about returning to her homeland it was proving far from straightforward logistically. There were no passenger boats during the six weeks following VE Day but they were due to start up during the week beginning the 25th June. Departures were scheduled for Tuesday, Thursday and Saturday mornings from Southampton. She had, of course, applied for the necessary permissions to return but had yet to hear back. As it happened, the timescale for her return lay firmly in the hands of her husband.

> Immigration Office,7, Pollet Street
> 28th June 1945

Dear Sir or Madam,

Kathleen Le Bargy has informed me that you will provide accommodation for him/her/them. As soon as I receive written confirmation of this, the issue of a permit to travel will be recommended.

Please confirm this as soon as possible by letter to Immigration Office, 7, Pollet, or preferably by telephone to Immigration Office 1561. When replying please quote No 824 to avoid any confusion.

Yours faithfully, PIERRE DE PUTRON, Immigration Officer.

---

5   See Exhibit E.

My father replied immediately and three weeks later received a telegram with the following news:

> 17th July 1945
> = HOME THURSDAY MORNING LOVE = KATH

On Thursday 19th July 1945 my mother boarded the ferry that would return her to her family and her homeland. She was older, wiser and sadder, but she had survived the years apart and so had they. Whether the love she and Charles felt for each other would hold strong enough to overcome the turbulence of those intervening years remained to be seen. But the signs were good and she could only hope.

The mood was one of excitement and highly-charged emotion as the boat lumbered across the English Channel carrying its cargo of expectant passengers back to their homes. The decks were packed full of evacuees as the boat made its final approach to the port and the familiar islands of Herm, Sark and Jethou came into view. The harbour was as beautiful as ever and the evacuees watched, mesmerised, as the memories of their past collided with the beauty of the present. People openly wept, for their loss and perhaps for their good fortune, but mostly to release the past and dare to hope for a better future.

Hundreds of people stood on the quay waving flags and shouting out their welcome for loved ones on board and, as the ropes were thrown and the ship was safely moored against the quay, the evacuees searched anxiously for familiar faces.

Mum's welcome party stood ready to receive her: Dad, Nan, Pop, Auntie Peg and her four children. Each with their own story to tell, or perhaps to keep quiet, and all standing ready now to wave and shout and cry their way back into each other's lives.

CHAPTER 9

The Aftermath

IN TIME MOST EVACUEES returned to Guernsey, but for many that prospect proved every bit as daunting as the original evacuation. As the community took steps towards reconciliation it had to make peace with a future that sometimes disapproved of its past. For some, the pain of reunion matched, or even surpassed, that of the initial separation. Fathers failed to recognise daughters, sons now called someone else "Mum" and newly formed families were once again torn apart, this time in the cause of peace.

Once the euphoria of the long-awaited reunion with family and friends had subsided, Mum began to struggle to settle back into island life. She and Dad had moved into Romo just a few weeks before she evacuated and, in the intervening years, she had dreamed of little else than of making Romo into a home for the two of them on her return. But the house she walked into in July 1945 seemed strange and unfamiliar to her. The cupboards were empty, the furniture had been moved around, the walls looked shabby and in need of fresh wallpaper and, worst of all, she and Dad were no longer living alone. It was now Betty's home too and Betty was in no hurry to move out.

The vastness of the English countryside had thrilled Mum, she had loved the liveliness of Bridgwater and the excitement of the surrounding towns and cities. Guernsey, by comparison, felt a little dull and lacklustre to her now. It seemed remote and isolated in ways she would never have considered before the war. There was no prospect of work, so the financial independence that the war had given her was lost, and she missed all the new friends and acquaintances that she had made in the UK.

Mum was not alone, many evacuees were deeply unsettled on their return. To exacerbate the problem the local community, that had shown such solidarity during the Occupation, sometimes failed to open its arms wide enough to embrace the returning refugees and make them feel sufficiently welcome. People who had once lived side by side now felt like strangers, and the returning islanders often felt like intruders in their own homes. Some went straight back to the mainland but most stuck it out and hoped that the mutual feelings of unease that they shared with those who had remained would eventually subside.

From time to time Mum's demeanour was a little sharp and off-hand in those first few months, especially towards Betty. She told Betty that she planned to run Romo as a guest house and that she would like her to move out so that she could offer her room to visitors. But Betty was young and in love and unaware of the urgency of her sister-in-law's request. It would be several years before she was ready to move out and it wasn't until 25th May 1952 that Mum was finally able to open up her house and welcome Mr and Mrs Sexton from Putney as her first ever guests.

Meanwhile, people all around her were also busy trying to rebuild their lives. Her two sisters had immersed themselves fully in the task of raising their expanding families; Dink now had three children and Peg six. Mum and Dad were left to face the fact that they were now unlikely to have a family of their own.

During the spring of 1954, they were given the opportunity to buy Romo. The post-war years had not proved easy for them, financially or emotionally, and taking on a mortgage was a big step. But they didn't hesitate. Mum started letting out all four of

Romo's bedrooms to help pay the mortgage and she and Dad took to sleeping in the lounge. Only when the last of the guests were settled upstairs for the night could they rest, mindful of the fact that they would need to rise early to pack the camp beds and all the bedding well out of sight before the first of their guests rose in the morning. It was a period of constant exhaustion but they considered it a small price to pay to secure a better future. As it happened, this particular arrangement did not last long.

In late autumn 1955, and with just a few months to go until her fortieth birthday, Mum discovered she was pregnant. My parents were thrilled at their unexpected good fortune and I was born safe and well on 23rd May the following spring. However, my arrival necessitated a change to the life style to which they had become accustomed. They would no longer be able to rent out all four of Romo's bedrooms to visitors, thus significantly reducing their disposable income. But perhaps most importantly, the regular trips that Mum had been making to the mainland since the end of the war, would now no longer be sustainable. She had never told her family or friends where, or for what reason, she was going, although she must have told my father as she had occasionally taken him with her.

CHAPTER 10

Romo

I HAVE A HOST of monochrome memories of growing up in Guernsey in the late 1950s, mostly courtesy of my father who was an avid photographer and who generally chose me as his subject. When the film on his camera was full he would disappear for hours on end into our kitchen-turned-dark room with his bewildering collection of potions and paraphernalia whilst I, despite my best attempts at protest, remained firmly excluded. Impatiently jealous of the time he spent without me, I would ride my tricycle round and round our tiny back yard until finally he would emerge, triumphant, and beckon me in to see the black and white prints, pegged out on a makeshift line to dry.

The photos told of a happy, straightforward childhood, full of innocence and love. The diary of the special relationship between a father and his only daughter. I sometimes wonder if my mother envied our closeness, if she ever felt excluded? If she did she never showed it, preferring instead to pour all her efforts into nurturing her small immediate family and supporting our extended one.

"Your father always hoped you would be a girl," she would tell me, smiling ruefully and leaving me to assume that she had always hoped for the same, which I did without question.

In the early 1960s, my father switched from taking black and white prints to photographic slides, and colour began painting our lives. I was approaching school age and my parents had prepared me well for the emotional challenges that lay ahead.

"I didn't cry at all," I announced proudly at the end of my first day, "but most of the boys did," and we laughed together, proud of the fact that I was taking it all in my stride.

This gentle nurturing and encouragement continued throughout my time in primary school. There was always a kiss goodbye, a welcome home hug and a bedtime story, and beyond that, I could pretty much choose whatever expression of love I wanted from them. They, in turn, remained the focus of my affection whilst I took those first tiny steps towards independence. For the time being at least, we could all relax in the knowledge that I would not yet look beyond them for truth, guidance and love.

And then, one spring day in 1962, my parents suddenly announced that we were going on holiday to Bournemouth. I was six years old and it was my first time away from home so I remember some aspects of it quite well. Like strolling through the beautifully manicured gardens in the centre of town and standing beside the river at Christchurch. I remember dining in the restaurant of the same posh hotel every night and the kindly waiter who summoned up beans on toast to satisfy my fussy eating habits. And I had a sense that my parents had a purpose, though I couldn't pinpoint what that purpose might have been.

On our return, Mum set about converting Romo into a "bed and breakfast" as she did every spring, and we prepared to welcome the annual stream of visitors into our lives. This meant our relocation from the main bedrooms on the first floor of the house to the two much smaller attic rooms which overlooked the harbour, affording our guests the relative luxury of the spacious first-floor bedrooms with their easier access to the single toilet situated on the landing nearby. It also heralded several months of hard work for my mother that inevitably tied her to the house more than she would have wanted.

I am sitting on my bed watching the gulls as they soar past my window; Daddy always says I am a daydreamer. I love my summer bedroom. High up in the attic it is like the land at the top of the Faraway Tree in the book Mummy and Daddy take turns to read to me at bedtime. Neither of them will ever skip a chapter because they can't bear to miss anything. So I hear everything through twice. But I don't mind, it is our family's favourite and I can never get enough of it.

My legs are aching from carrying all my books and games up the steep stairs. My winter bedroom is almost empty, soon it will be ready for the first visitors who are due to arrive next week. I feel very grown-up as I arrange my books on their new shelves and pack my games away into different cupboards. It is the first year I have been trusted to do this by myself.

This year, there are two beds in my room and I am sure there is usually only one. They are placed alongside each other, up against the wall, so I have to climb over them both to reach the shelves. Mine must be the one closest to the wall because my pyjamas and teddy are tucked under the mismatch of blankets and the stiff white sheet that mum has pulled tightly around them. But the other bed is made up too?

"Jackie? Jackie? JACKIE!" Dad is shouting up the stairs.

"Yes?"

"Can you come down here a minute?" It is not a question.

He is waiting for me at the bottom of the stairs and I launch myself into his arms. Skilfully he swings me around, channelling the momentum to make sure that I don't hit the walls as he sweeps me into the lounge and throws me down onto the sofa. Mum is already in the room, she is wearing a sky blue dress with a white pinny tied neatly around her waist. She waits, standing, for Dad to pull his armchair up close. As he sits she sits too, next to me but not touching, her hands in her lap, her fingers straying to the edges of the pinny, to pick at its lace.

As an only child, I am used to their undivided attention but this feels strange. As if they have something important to tell me but are afraid for me to hear it.

"How are you getting on darling? Do you need help moving your things?" She sounds genuinely concerned but, even at six years old, I sense this is not the purpose of the conversation.

"It's going fine thanks".

They exchange glances and, perhaps as agreed, it is Dad who then speaks …

"We're going to be extra busy for the next few months sweetheart. Mummy does such a good job looking after all our visitors that even more than usual want to come to stay with us this year."

This is good news for me, if not for my mum. I love having people to stay, especially if they bring children that I can play with. But wait, there is more …

"Now … this is nothing for you to worry about … but Mummy and I have decided that she could really do with some help …"

"Yes! I really do need help darling. You understand that don't you? Do you remember we went to meet a girl when we were on holiday? Well, she is coming over to give me a hand. It will be lovely won't it darling? A bit like having an older sister for you because she will have to sleep in your room with you. You don't mind do you, darling?" Mummy is barely pausing for breath as she trips over words she is too eager to speak.

Daddy is watching me closely, gauging my reaction.

"How long will she be staying?" I ask cautiously, searching their faces for what they are not telling me.

"Well, let's wait and see. The most important thing is that we make her feel welcome here. It will be very strange for her, *suddenly living with us and all that. You do understand don't you darling?"*

I have never seen Mum this animated and I surrender myself totally to her excitement as I edge towards her and feel her arms envelop me. But as I cuddle into her, and Dad smiles on fondly, I feel a strong sense of caution lingering in the air, and I am not at all sure that I do fully understand …

The next day the three of us went down to the harbour to meet her. She arrived on the mailboat, waving and full of smiles as she descended the gangplank carrying a single cream suitcase. Mum approached her first, welcoming her with open arms. But the hug, though genuine, seemed stiff and awkward. After shyly embracing my father the girl turned her attention to me. She paused for a moment, as if she were assessing what she might be allowed to do, and then she grabbed hold of my hand and marched me off along the quay.

The bed that had been placed for her beside mine brought both of us comfort at night. She was warm and wholesome and it felt good to widen our family home so that, for a while, three became four. She had come to help Mum with the visitors but sometimes, when she was finished, we would take her with us to show her around the island. Occasionally, she was sent to meet me from school. Those were the times I loved the best, when I could fling myself at her and claim her for my own as we walked hand in hand back to our home.

Our happiness, like the trees all around us, burst with the vigour and promise of spring. But gradually it died with the heat of the summer and fell away with the leaves as soon as autumn arrived. Suddenly she and Mum seemed always at odds, leaving Dad in the middle trying to maintain the peace. The bed next to me was left empty at night and, before long, Romo became home to just the three of us again.

Did she ever whisper her secrets to me?

I still try to listen. But all I can hear is the echo of silence in a bedroom we once shared.

She had worked for us as a chambermaid and lived with us as a family member, and suddenly she was neither. The tears that had slowly been destroying the equilibrium of our family were, in part, stilled when she left. And so, although I had loved her, I embraced with some relief the tenuous harmony that was restored in our home; a harmony that was to erase all memory of her for nearly half a century.

CHAPTER 11

You Will Miss Me When I'm Gone

WHEN I WAS FOURTEEN we moved away from town to a bungalow in the southern parish of St Martins. It was a much smaller house than Romo and this suited my parents, and their retirement plans, well. There would be less maintenance and more time for them to relax and enjoy life. It did not, however, suit me. My mother had long since given up running Romo as a guest house and I had grown accustomed to having lots of space for entertaining my friends. There were ugly tears as I lashed out, selfishly, but inevitably our last day in Romo came and went without the world ending as I had predicted.

Just before we left my parents sat me down and told me about Michael, my baby brother who had died following bowel surgery. Had I not cried inconsolably for our loss they might have told me more, but they were always a little too eager to protect me from heartache. In any case, though I had reached an age where they felt it their duty to tell me, it was clearly a wound they had no wish to reopen. They belonged to a generation that had been saved from despair by its stiff upper lip, they had no intention of indulging in self-pity now.

It was the start of the 1970s and I was beginning to take control of my independence. Mum's attempts to slow me down fell on predictably deaf ears and I pushed the boundaries by staying out as late as I could get away with. Like most mothers she worried constantly and, like most children, I never felt I gave her any cause for concern.

On leaving school, I spent four years at university in Southampton and returned to Guernsey with a degree and a teaching qualification which enabled me to take up a job as a maths teacher in a local secondary school. But neither marriage nor a stressful job could tame me and it wasn't until I became pregnant with my first child that I learnt to put my own life on hold and concentrate on the needs of others. Neither of my parents had ever put pressure on me to conform to a particular path in life. The support they had given me, at every stage, was so quietly selfless that I had seldom even appreciated it was there. I had never stopped to consider whether my mother might like grandchildren, but she called to my father with such excitement when I rang to tell her the news that I was genuinely touched. She fussed over me relentlessly throughout my first pregnancy which I considered wholly unnecessary, and when Anneka arrived she lit up her world in ways I could never have imagined.

"Whatever did we do before we had you to look at?" she would ask her, and suddenly I understood my mother so much better, because Anneka lit up my world too. It was then that we became close as mother and daughter, embracing that one final opportunity, just in time.

I had always known how much I was 'wanted' and there was no escaping the fact that having a baby at the age of 40 was highly unusual, and far from ideal, in the 1950s. Even so, I had rarely given much thought to my mum's experience of motherhood or how she might have been feeling during her childless years. Anneka's birth brought joy and hope to us all, but it was also a painful reminder that Mum had lost her first born and I found myself constantly focussing on that death, unable to imagine anything worse.

Mum was never one to dwell on the past but, very occasionally, we talked of the years that had passed between Michael and me, of how she had always wished for a large family, and of how unexpected my arrival had been all those years later. It was around those three simple facts that I wove my web of misunderstanding, aided no doubt, by her determination to conceal the secrets that underpinned the mystery.

It shames me now to think that we left so much unsaid, but the reality was that neither of us was comfortable with the sharing of intimate details. Her intolerance of any form of nostalgia or highly-charged emotion always seemed to me a direct criticism of my inability to hide my feelings. It meant that I never really felt I could open up to her. Or perhaps I simply sensed the dangers of navigating a river that ran so unfathomably deep it could have swept us both away in a heartbeat.

In July 1988 Mum had what Dad described as a "funny turn". The doctor diagnosed a mild stroke from which, he predicted, she would make a complete recovery, and she and Dad insisted I did not cancel our impending camping holiday in France. I felt anxious about leaving her, but the daily phone calls home were reassuring at first, until one day it was my dad who answered.

"I'm afraid Mum has been taken into hospital. I think you had better come home."

We were in the south of France at the time. Knowing it must be serious for my dad to call me back we set out immediately for the long drive home. Many hours of thought and worry later I found myself at her bedside. She looked better than I was expecting. Her eyes blue and sparkling. Thrilled to see me.

"Hello, darling. How was your trip? You needn't have come home just for me."

"Of course I needed to come home, Mum."

"But you really needed a holiday, my love. You work so hard."

"You are much more important than my holiday, Mum, I wanted to see you. How are you feeling?"

As if on cue a nurse bristled into the bay, interrupting our conversation before mum had a chance to reply.

"Mrs Le Bargy's daughter? I need you to come with me please ..."

A look of panic fleetingly crossed Mum's face. She needn't have worried.

"Of course. But could you give me a few minutes with her please. I've only just arrived."

But the nurse was on a mission and protest was useless. As she ushered me out of the bay I turned back towards my mother, who looked anxious now and puzzled at this unexpected intrusion.

"I'll be right back Mum. You have a rest now."

The nurse led me out of the ward and into a long corridor where I could just about make out a familiar figure, pacing the floor anxiously, at the far end. As I walked towards her, Val opened her arms wide, but the hug was brief.

"Hi, Jack. We've managed to book a doctor's appointment for you so that he can tell you about your mum. We need to go straight to the surgery. He will be able to fill you in on everything." She took hold of my arm and led me briskly outside to where Auntie Dink was waiting in her car with the engine running. During the brief journey to the surgery, none of us spoke. Small talk seemed irrelevant and I couldn't bring myself to ask questions because I didn't want to hear the answers.

"We thought your mum had a minor stroke at first," our family doctor began, looking at me kindly, he knew us all well. "We've carried out lots of tests and scans ... and I'm very sorry to have to tell you ..."

He was used to delivering bad news. He understood the magnitude of the moment for me and his responsibility to give me all the facts. But I wasn't used to receiving it and, though I was in the surgery for a good thirty minutes, I caught only a handful of words.

"… cancer … spread everywhere … nothing we can do …"

I felt numb as I left the building. The day was grey and overcast and I felt the chill of winter rather than the warmth of that late summer's day. Auntie Dink and Val stood waiting, ready to intercept my emotions and channel them down their predetermined path. They already knew, of course, and Auntie Dink was quick to jump in.

"You mustn't tell her Jackie! I know her better than anyone and I am absolutely certain that she wouldn't want to know. We just need to do everything we can to make sure that whatever time she has left is as happy and as comfortable as possible"

Wait a minute. Mum didn't know?! How could that be right?

"Think about it, Jack." Val sensed I was wavering. "Would you want to know? I certainly wouldn't. Wouldn't you just want to enjoy the time you have left? It's really important that you don't tell her."

They dropped me home with firm instructions to pull myself together before visiting her again. I felt as if I had been thrust into battle with no means of defence, abandoned and left blinded by the terror of what lay ahead. But they were right in a way. I did need to pull myself together because the future was far from certain and I needed to summon up sufficient courage with which to face it.

— — —

"Lovely!" she said biting into the soft flesh of the gorged fruit. "You can't beat a ripe plum."

Thick, purple juice oozed out of each bite and trickled down her face, leaving a sticky, sweet trail. I knew they were her favourite. I cleaned her up and settled onto the bed beside her.

"So how are you feeling Mum?"

Her eyes clouded a little. There was a brief hesitation. And then, wearily, she started, as if her heart were heavy with a load she was desperate to lighten. …

"Well, actually it's good that you've come because the doctor has just left."

"Oh?"

"Yes. I asked him to explain what was wrong with me."

The air stuck in my lungs, refusing to move. My heart was racing, begging me to breathe.

"He sat on my bed …" she continued … "and held my hand. We talked for a long time. He was so very kind."

We had reached the final leg of the relay and she was passing the baton on to me, urging me to run with it, but still the words wouldn't come. What did he tell you, Mum? I needed to face it, needed to be brave. But this was too much, too soon. And then she looked directly into my eyes and she knew it too. She had given me a chance that I was not yet ready to take. And so she placed her needs aside, just as she had always done, and turned instead towards mine.

"Now then Darling, how is Anneka? How did she get on with the camping?"

The truth hung heavy in the air between us that evening as we gave normality our best attempt. Immoveable, intractable truth, audaciously heartless in the midst of so much love.

The next day she had all but passed, the chance she had given me gone. The end was mercifully quick but I was at least able to tell her how much I loved her. And I knew that she heard me as a single tear rolled down her cheek.

Mum's sudden passing left me totally unprepared for the years that lay ahead without her and thus ensured that I would never fully get over losing her. All the milestones on my own journey through motherhood would now be faced without the one person that I would most want to share them with. She had lit up my path and guided me, for as long as she had been able, but in the end, she had no choice but to leave me. Though I had considered her predictable in life she would surprise me in death in ways I could never have imagined. I had lost her before I had learnt to appreciate or truly understand her and she had always known it because, in the end, she was right;

"You will miss me when I'm gone".

CHAPTER 12

Letting Go

JUST AS SHE HAD let me go as I grew from child to adult, selflessly and without question, I now had to let her go. But I did so reluctantly and without the good grace that she had somehow mustered all those years previously. I had failed to give her credit for knowing me so well but still she was prepared to give me one last chance. In the days of grief that followed, her young and carefree spirit whispered to me often, as I cleaned her husband's home and rewrote my role in his life. As she sang and danced around me I thought how alike we were, what fun we might have, and I imagined we might be friends forever. But after the funeral she left me, before I could catch my breath, and dancing all the while to the tune of my lost opportunity. Many times, over the years, I tried to summon her back, but it was almost a lifetime before she finally returned.

It was hard to see my dad, once part of my special two, on his own, and even harder to leave him that way. But the weather was kind, and the mild autumn days that followed her death helped to sedate our pain. Our father-daughter bond remained strong but, by mutual consent, we did not branch out into territories that we had not yet fully explored together. Dad continued to keep his feelings tightly in check, it was the hallmark of his generation and I expected nothing less. And, for his sake, I tried my best to do the same. Still, I visited him often to show him my love and to keep him company in case he felt lonely. Messages of support flooded in from family and friends and also from people I didn't even know and it felt good to know that Mum, and indeed our compact family unit, had been very much loved.

I am sitting in my father's lounge, it is a few days after Mum's funeral. He is on the phone but soon he will turn his attention to me. I have never really had to share him, it is perhaps the only benefit I have found in being an only child, so I don't anticipate having to wait long.

It is good to hear him talking animatedly after the great sadness that has overwhelmed our world. But I can't quite make out who he is talking to. In the flicker of his eyes, I sense concern, directed towards me perhaps? I rise slowly out of my chair, weary from a long day at school, to go into the kitchen to make us a cup of tea. A signal to him that it is okay to continue his call.

Our tea is brewed yet still his conversation flows without me. I pass him his cup and settle down on the settee at the far end of the room. I feel jaded after the emotional upheaval of the past few weeks. The tea is refreshing and welcome. I pick up the local newspaper in a mindless attempt to catch up with the current goings-on but it is hard to ignore what is happening in the room. I glance across at Dad, his attention lost to the ebb and flow of the call. He listens intently before responding with concern and then listening again.

She (I am sure now it is a she) is not one of his friends. His tone is too benevolent, almost paternal. And she is someone he cares deeply about, that much is clear.

"Who was that?" I ask when he finally replaces the receiver.

But, in my eagerness to engage with my father, I forget to listen to his answer.

When my second child was born we named him Charles. My father was thrilled. As the young Charles grew stronger with each passing month, the old Charles began to weaken and fade. In the autumn of 1995 emphysema finally robbed him of his independence and he came to live with us for a short while before being taken into hospital for twenty-four-hour care.

Dad passed away on 17th December 1995 after many years of not living life to the full. Not once did I ever hear him complain and he embraced his death as he lived his life, with dignity and resignation. The final balance in his bank account on the day that he died was £36,579, a number that is etched in my memory. Not for its magnitude, though, but for the fact that it was also his telephone number. It was clearly his time and, in his own words, he had enjoyed a good innings. And so my special people were gone but would never be forgotten leaving me to bring up my own children without the priceless umbrella of support that their love and guidance would have given.

It was my husband, Pete, who sorted Dad's house after he died, and packed my parents' lives away in four large removals boxes because the task proved too daunting for me. For years I took comfort in the fact that the boxes lay, out of sight, in our attic. It wasn't that I imagined they contained anything exceptional, I simply felt that my parents lived on in them whilst their contents remained untouched. I had already lost them too soon and had no wish to lose them again.

Every now and then, Pete would gently try to coax me into dealing with their contents. Mostly he was unsuccessful, but on one occasion I agreed. Familiarity greeted me as I opened the first box and removed a couple of ornaments. Tacky though they had always seemed to me, I knew immediately that I could never throw them away. They were the chosen keepsakes of lives now passed and, though they would never again occupy their special place on one particular mantelpiece, there would always be room for them in my heart.

Beneath the ornaments lay a medium-sized blue quilted box tightly clasped shut with a tiny brass hook. Inside I found lots of green wooden houses and fewer red ones, a shiny top hat and various crumpled bank notes, the sight of which brought the memories flooding back. Dad and I had mostly played draughts and chess, but our favourite was always Monopoly if we had the time. We would lay the game out on a table between our two armchairs, me perched on the edge of mine in mock concentration, him lounging cross-legged in his, relaxed and easy. Puffing on his pipe. Giving me a chance. Our house had no heating other than an open fire in the living room, but I never remember feeling cold. Summer or winter there was always the comfort of a freshly-cooked meal on the table and the safety of our small family unit, it was all the warmth that I needed.

Under the Monopoly board lay a carefully folded, well-worn, navy blue Guernsey jumper. I lifted the garment carefully out of the box and buried my head in its wool. It smelt musty from years of neglect but somehow it still carried the essence of him.

I am 8, or maybe 9, years old and I feel the chill of winter as I lie in bed in my "winter bedroom". The blankets weigh heavy as I pull them around me, we have no heating upstairs. Dad is sitting on my bed wearing a Guernsey, his traditional line of defence against the aggressive cold of winter. He has come to tuck me in, as he does every night, and I am asking:

"Why do I not have any brothers and sisters Daddy? I wish I had one."

And suddenly I am listening hard, though I have missed some of the details because Dad is telling me something he has never told me before. Perhaps I have worn him down with my constant questioning? Or perhaps he had already decided that tonight was the right time ...

"You do have one darling. You do. Don't you remember?"

"I do?"

"Yes, sweetheart. Surely you remember all the arguments? She was so unhappy she ran away."

And I can't remember, but I can imagine her running, to the top of Bosq Lane, along the Canichers and through the tiny cobbled lane that leads to my Auntie Dink's house. She is running as fast as she can away from our family and it is too much to bear. How could anyone not love my parents?

"It was your mum and I that she was angry with, darling. It wasn't your fault."

But I am inconsolable. Why would anyone want to run away from us?

Dad had not expected this rush of tears and, as he gently brushed them aside, he coaxed me away from our past and back into the cool darkness of my winter bedroom. And with that, we buried her, deep in our souls, and out of reach of all but the most persistent enquiry.

PART TWO

The Bailiwick of Guernsey comprises a number of islands each with its own identity and charm. One gem in this archipelago in the English Channel is the tiny island of Sark. Just three miles long by one-and-a-half miles wide, cars are not permitted, and Sark must be negotiated on foot, by bicycle or by horse and cart. The politics are controversial, the economy fragile, yet the peace and tranquillity are intoxicating.

A hidden treasure lying on the south coast of Sark is the Venus Pool. None but the most persistent will find it and none but the most intrepid will access it. The signs tantalise their followers by abandoning them at the nearby silver mines. Alone and remote, most give up at this point, but those that persevere will be well-rewarded for their efforts. The pool is surrounded by rocky outcrops from which the brave and the foolhardy, emboldened by onlookers, can launch themselves into the murky depths below.

During my one and only visit to the pool, I found it unnervingly easy to jump. The noisy encouragement from friends and family, the thrill of the feat and the velvety welcome that awaited below lured me to the very limits of my bravery. Higher and higher I climbed, each time checking cautiously before the commitment. A simple stumble or miscalculation would have changed the course of my life forever, but the thrill when I got it right was marvellous.

CHAPTER 1

Parallel Universe

AN ARMY OF CLOUDS, swift and disciplined, scudded overhead as I walked along the beach. Row upon row of the chiselled white sculptures, for as far as the eye could see, marching across the velvet blue of the sky. Ahead of me our black labrador puppy, Mali, was splashing happily in the waves. Vazon Beach, first thing in the morning, was our special time.

Vazon is Guernsey's largest beach; a vast, untamed horseshoe of golden sand punctuated by a single rocky outcrop in the middle of the bay. An imposing granite seawall sweeps around half the perimeter before gradually giving way to rolling sand dunes at our end. Even in the cold darkness of mid-winter, an early morning walk was enough of a tonic to set me up for the day ahead. But on a glorious morning such as this a stroll on the sand, beside an ocean tamed by the arrival of summer, was inspirational.

On leaving the beach my pace quickened and my mind started racing towards the day ahead. Were my lessons adequately planned? Was my marking up to date? Where was that spare calculator I needed to take to school? After many years teaching, I felt relaxed and comfortable in the role but mindful, too, of the weight of its responsibility. Success in the classroom depends on meticulous organisation and planning, even the slightest oversight can result in catastrophe.

After a short walk inland from the coast, we reached our

19th-century fisherman's cottage that Pete had spent the previous two years renovating. The east-facing facade remained largely untouched, and gave no hint of the substantial extension that wrapped around the back of the property. I loved how the dark cosiness of the old cottage contrasted with the light and airy feel of the new build. From the dark wooden frames in the old part to the bright modern collages in the new, it was a home packed full of the flow of our lives, a celebration of all those we loved.

As I crossed the road to enter the drive, the grains of glassy quartz in the granite sparkled like diamonds in the glow of the morning sun. Mali strained on the lead, urging me to hurry, mindful of the breakfast that awaited her. But I had a more urgent matter to attend to and pulled her to a stop beneath the first floor, low-level window on the gable end. Reaching up I knocked sharply on one of the tiny glass panes several times.

"Charlie? Charlie! Are you awake?"

"CHARLIE?! It's seven o'clock. Can you get up!"

Though naturally bright and talented, our youngest son was not known for his compliance with any matter educational. It would often take many attempts to get him up and ready for school.

Within an hour, however, I had managed to persuade him out of bed, out of the house and into the car. For once, it seemed, we might be on time.

As I turned the key in the ignition I launched into the first of the questions on my morning agenda. Barely awake, Charlie let out a groan. But this was my quality time with my fourteen-year-old son and I was determined to make the most of it. Later in the day, he would make his own way home on the school bus, and in the evening we would lose him to his guitar and his all-consuming world of music. But here in the car, first thing in the morning, there were things we needed to sort. As a teacher in his school, I needed to at least try to help him comply with his teachers' wishes, for all our sakes.

On arrival at school, we went our separate ways, but I knew he would bring me his smile at lunchtime when he was hungry for something from the canteen, and his pockets were empty.

An orderly progression of students passed through my classroom door that morning, their transit timed to the sound of a bell that organised our lives into fifty-minute slots. This Pavlovian response, replicated to perfection throughout the school, generally ensured that the institution ran smoothly. And then, finally, the bell took a rest and afforded us all the luxury of eating our lunch in peace.

The afternoon saw my A-level students sitting their final exam of the season and, just before it was due to finish, I went along to the examination hall to greet them. The buzz of excitement, relief and disappointment formed an explosion of sound as the doors opened and the students were released. Like a magnet, I drew them around me one last time to hear how difficult they had found the paper and to take this final opportunity to say goodbye. It is a privilege to teach, and I had become fond of these wonderful young people; I wanted to wish them well on their onward journeys through life. Little did I know that my own journey was just about to take a most unexpected turn.

The academic year still had several weeks to run but the hard work was over, at least for the moment, and the prospect of the Guernsey summer that lay ahead brought a smile as I drove home that afternoon. The driveway behind our cottage was empty when I arrived and the only greeting that awaited me was from Mali, quivering with excitement at seeing me and the prospect of a nice long walk. But she would have to wait. I put the kettle on, swapped my work clothes for beach wear and switched on the computer. Our family desktop dealt with all of our digital needs and there would be the inevitable queue for access later on.

I made a cup of tea and sipped on it gratefully as I lounged back in the chair and waited for the inbox to fill. The internet was running slowly but I was in no hurry. When the emails arrived they were mostly spam, but towards the bottom of the screen, one from Friends Reunited caught my attention. The sender was a Charley Miller and the name seemed familiar? I hesitated for a moment before making the connection. Charley Miller had requested my friendship on Facebook last week! With no profile picture, however, and no information other than that she was female and that she lived in London, the request had seemed too dodgy to accept. Now she was emailing me!

I took a deep breath and considered what to do. What harm could there be in reading an email? I wouldn't be committing myself to anything and Friends Reunited, as far as I knew, was a reputable site. In true puppy style, Mali lay crashed at my feet. There was no immediate urgency to take her for a walk.

I took a moment to look around the room. Photographs and mementoes, of loved ones past and present, covered the walls and packed the shelves. I was in my home and I felt safe. Impulsively, I clicked on her name and the email sprang triumphantly to life, uncurling itself with a flourish before splashing its message across the screen.

I paused. Deliberately.

As if I might still have something to lose.

But caution was already giving way to curiosity. Who was this Charley Miller from London, and why was she still trying to contact me? It could be a scam or it could be something really important. Either way I needed to know.

Hi,

I'm trying to find relatives of Michele Le Bargy, I'm her granddaughter and I am trying, in particular, to trace her sister Jacqueline.

Michele and Jacqueline's father was called Charles and they had a brother called Martin.

I would appreciate it if you could get back to us as it has taken several years to find any Le Bargy.

I look forward to hearing from you.

Charley

Something deep within me stirred. For a long time, I sat, dazed, chasing shadowy thoughts that refused to be caught. I read the message through again, slowly this time, scrutinising each word, checking in case I had missed something.

It had to be me. Le Bargy is a Guernsey name, but very unusual even on the island. There was no other Jacqueline Le Bargy in Guernsey, of that I was certain.

"Surely you remember?" a voice in my head was whispering, "Isn't this what you have always been waiting for?"

———

The tide was lazily advancing across the sand when I found myself once again walking along the seashore with Mali. The beach had attracted a large crowd that day and many had lingered, with their loved ones, to enjoy the last warmth of the sun's rays. It was a good few hours until sunset but it promised to be spectacular. Not a cloud remained in our Guernsey sky to smother its magic.

I found a quiet spot on the beach and sat down. A rest would be good for Mali's young legs and I needed time to think. Charley's email had thrilled me and ignited a chain of crazy thoughts that were challenging my powers of reason. I had settled on a considered reply to her, one that cautiously invited further contact. However excited I felt, I was also acutely aware that disappointment often lingers in the wanting of something too much. The sand all around me was hot, dry and silky smooth as I swept it up in handfuls and watched it slip silently through my fingers. Like the thoughts that I couldn't hold on to, no matter how hard I tried; a thousand grains lost to the eternity of each moment.

As I left the coast road and turned back into our lane I suddenly felt cold. Time had passed unnoticed and I had no watch for reference. Pete's car was in the drive but subconsciously I had prepared myself well for his probing.

"Where have you been? I was getting really worried! Charlie and I have eaten and yours is in the oven." And before I could answer ... "Did you see that there was an email for you on Friends Reunited?"

"Yes, I did thanks."

"Who's Charley Miller and what was that all about?"

"I have no idea. She requested me as a friend on Facebook last week but I declined as I don't know her. I've sent her a quick email but I'm not expecting it will amount to anything."

My tone was calculated, nonchalant even, and it seemed I had judged it well. For the busy day-to-day bustle of our everyday existence pushed on with its own agenda, ensuring that this particular fingerprint in time was done and dusted, at least for the moment.

Throughout the week that followed I checked our emails at every opportunity. Each time waiting, impatiently, for the inbox to fill and hoping for a reply from Charley that never came. Perhaps it was fate that she had not replied? Or perhaps the technology had let me down? I could find no trace of my reply to her, might it simply have disappeared into the ether? Either way, I wanted no regrets. So, early on Saturday morning, while the rest of my family was still snuggled in sleep, I decided to give it one more try.

I reread Charley's email before replying with one simple sentence asking where she was living. I felt sure that even the briefest message from me would elicit a response from her if the original request had been genuine. I checked that the message had been sent and, satisfied that I had now done everything I could, I walked away from the computer and resolved to get on with my weekend. This time the response was immediate but it remained unseen until much later in the day.

Hi Jag,

Thank you so much for your reply.
I am living in London, England.

Are you able to help me at all with my search?

Michele and Jacqueline's mother was called Katherine and their brother's name was Peter not Martin.

I hope you can be of help. We have been trying to find Jacqueline for many years.

Charley.

The tiny clues emboldened me, my mother's name was Kathleen, not Katherine, and my husband's name was Peter; perhaps she meant brother-in-law rather than brother? It was almost enough. I was starting to dream and the water beckoned, all the while urging me higher and higher, very soon I would be tempted to jump.

By now it was late afternoon and we were due to go to some friends for an early evening BBQ. Charlie needed to be fed and delivered to a friend's house, and Pete and I had yet to sort out our contribution to the evening ahead. Nevertheless, I judged that I had just about enough time to squeeze in a quick reply.

Hi Charley,

I might be able to help you but since this is all rather out of the blue could you answer a few questions for me first, please?

When did Michele last see Jacqueline? How old are they both?

Also, do you have any more information about Peter?

Looking forward to hearing from you and maybe being able to help.

Jag

As I pressed "send" I picked up the precious fragments of possibility, enough now, I judged, to be shared. For the first time I shared my hopes with Pete and we took the story with us to entertain our friends. The evidence was undeniably flimsy, but the emails had generated in me a strong sense of mystery from the past, and that made the story far more compelling. Somehow, the notion of a brother or sister had lain buried, at the back of my mind, for decades I had simply never found sufficient justification to express it. Charley's email was giving me that justification.

By the time we arrived home, late that night, I knew that sleep would not tempt me until I had checked for a reply in our inbox. This time it didn't disappoint. But the message, though sent from the same email address as before, was from someone other than Charley.

Hi Jag,

My name is Sharon, I am Michele's daughter and Charley's mum.

I'm sorry we have contacted you out of the blue. I know that mum has a sister and a brother but I don't know very much else I'm afraid.

I have done a little detective work myself at the registry in Kew and I did find their birth records.

My mum, Michele, was born on 15th January 1945 in Bournemouth and her sister, Jacqueline, was born on 12th November 1942 in Newton Abbott.

I have not managed to find a birth record yet for Peter.
Mum seems to think she was born in Guernsey, and she certainly seems to know a lot about St Peter Port.

If you could help in any way I would be most grateful.

Sharon

Life weaves its intriguing paths and sometimes we have no choice but to follow, trusting in its judgement and hoping that it will lead us to the truth. Disappointment threatened to overwhelm me. I had been lured by similarity and beguiled by coincidence but now I was certain that, however much I wanted it, this could not be my story.

In January 1945 my parents, though married, were living apart. Mum was an evacuee living in Bridgwater with her sister, whilst Dad was living with his mum and sister under Nazi Occupation in Guernsey. They had not seen each other for nearly 5 years, so there was no possibility that Michele could be my sister. Nor could I be the Jacqueline whom they were seeking because I was born in Guernsey in 1956.

I had awoken from the dream of a past that held such promise for the future. It had been too much to expect that life would bring me a sibling after all these years and, in my parallel universe, I was already grieving my loss. Possibility had beckoned for the briefest of moments, but what a relief it was, that hope had always lingered a pace or two behind, ever mindful of the need not to jump too soon.

CHAPTER 2

The Jigsaw of Life

THE NEXT DAY WAS Father's Day and, with my two stepsons now fathers themselves, it was a good cause for celebration in our family. We had planned to meet on the beach for a late afternoon BBQ. I slept pretty well considering the mixed emotions of the previous night and when I awoke the sun had already completed its onslaught through our bedroom and was busy nosing its way into our lounge. I filled the kettle and switched on the computer, placing all thoughts of preparations for our beach party furthest from my mind. I had unfinished business from the night before to attend to first.

Disappointment had given way to curiosity overnight and the caffeine gave a welcome boost as I sat myself down at the computer to pen my response to Sharon. It took a surprisingly long time before I was satisfied with the content and tone of the reply and, more than once, I had to stop myself from reaching out to the hope of further possibility. However much my heart wished it, this could not be my story and the best outcome I could expect was an intriguing brush with coincidence.

Hi Sharon,

Thanks for the info. I'm not sure that I can help but I will try.

My name is Jacqueline, my dad was Charles and my mum Kathleen and I am married to Peter! However, this all seems to be just a coincidence because I was born in Guernsey in 1956 and I am an only child (though I did have a brother, Michael, who died as a baby well before I was born). Le Bargy is an unusual name and my dad had two sisters so the name died out on that side of the family. Apart from that there is one other Le Bargy family in Guernsey, a cousin of my dad's.

Is your mum still alive and if so is she able to provide any further information that might help you? I'm wondering when they all lost contact with each other and why? How reliable is your detective work? Are you sure your mum was born in Bournemouth or do you think she may have been born in Guernsey?

My parents lived apart from 1940-1945 as mum evacuated to England at the start of the second world war but Dad stayed in Guernsey under German Occupation. So I'm afraid that your Jacqueline can't possibly be me, but I am interested in this and I will help you if I can.

Jag

Before I had time to relax back in my seat the immediacy of the reply pulled me straight back to the screen.

Was your mother's maiden name Loveridge?

A tiny shock, like the unexpected jolt from static, trickled down my throat and made it difficult to swallow. As I read and reread the message my concentration ebbed and flowed around the familiarity of the name.

Yes

Did she run a bed and breakfast in St Peter Port called Romo?

I looked at the screen, too stunned to move. The past was starting to reassemble in front of me and seemed intent on placing itself on a collision course with the future. I waited so long to reply that I thought I might have lost them, but I needn't have worried because, of course, they were waiting too.

Yes

Well, my Mum (Michele) used to work in that guest house

The mistake we all make is to believe that our history is in the past. It lives and breathes and follows us, desperate to be of relevance and, just occasionally, its patience is rewarded. There was not yet any clear picture and too many pieces were yet to be found, but slowly and surely parts of the jigsaw were simultaneously falling apart and starting to reassemble.

We are sitting on the floor in my summer bedroom with our backs up against her bed. She shakes the little glass pot furiously, before slamming it down into the palm of her free hand, once, twice, three times, as if she is trying to dislodge something. Gently, but firmly she takes my hand and strokes my nails with the tiny brush. Blood red, shiny and inexpertly applied, the varnish is too gaudy for a child, but I don't mind. I am six years old and I adore her.

The attic room is hot and sticky and our beds are pushed so closely to each other that, if I need the bathroom in the middle of the night, I have to climb over her first. We whisper our secrets into the early hours and I love her sleeping next to me. She is like the big sister that I have always longed for and, I hope that one day she might actually become my sister.

But sometimes her bed is empty and I worry where she might be ...

All too soon the cameo moment fades and the next time I look into my attic bedroom she is no longer there.

Hello, are you still there?

It's very confusing I know and I'm sorry to spring this on you, I hope you are ok?

Mum is still alive but for reasons we don't understand she isn't really interested in our search. We do know, from photos, that she visited her father in Guernsey when he was dying and that she met up with her sister Jackie and her niece who is a redhead. Her sister Jackie is a teacher.

But I'm confused, too, because the dates don't add up and you don't seem to know who mum is. Would you have known of Michele growing up and do you remember her visiting you in the mid-1990s?

Sharon

Somehow it was mid-morning and I was no longer alone. Sat next to me, excitedly sipping on a cup of tea was Anneka, her red hair shining in the sunlight that was now streaming in through the side window of the cottage. As I sat back to pause for breath, she reached across me to read the latest message on the screen. A cup of hot coffee had been placed in front of me alongside one that had long since gone cold. Behind me, Pete was leaning forwards over my chair, also trying to read the words on the screen. The dog was settled under my feet, oblivious to the emotions of those above her and Charlie was nowhere to be seen, presumably he was still asleep upstairs.

Had I met Michele in the mid-1990s as Sharon and Charley believed? I thought back to the autumn of 1995 when Dad was in hospital. I had spent a lot of time with him, helping with his meals and generally keeping him company. I tried to imagine the busy comings and goings of visitors to the ward. Had our paths crossed in the corridors of the hospital maybe? Had Dad mentioned anything about her to me, however small? I was at the very edge of reason with still some way to go but, try as I might, I could not push back any further.

Pete was cheering me on, Anneka was urging caution, but it was all just about enough. Though I had to agree with Anneka that much of what they had said could quickly have been found on family research sites, no search engine could possibly have known of a guest house called Romo that had long since been buried in anonymity. As my loved ones held their breath I penned my reply.

Hi, Yes I am still here and I'm also very confused. My name is Jackie and I am a teacher and I have a daughter with red hair. Please can I phone you?

Of course! We would be very happy to hear from you.
And by the way, my mum named my sister after you ...
her name is Jacqueline too ...

CHAPTER 3

In Search of Reality

"HELLO, JAG! I'M SORRY to have caused you all this confusion. I hope we haven't upset you?" It was Sharon who answered my call, and her voice immediately put me at ease. She sounded gentle and kind; understanding of the significance of this moment to us both, and excited to have found me.

"Don't worry, I'm fine. I'm really pleased you've contacted me … I'm just finding it hard to get my head around it all."

"I totally understand. It must be such a shock for us to be contacting you out of the blue like this."

We both had so many questions that conversation flowed easily, an hour passed, maybe two. It was a courtship of sorts as we ducked and weaved our way through our collective past.

"We think Mum was brought up in Guernsey because she often spoke about it, and she often spoke about you, too." Sharon told me kindly, but I sensed a deep sadness in her as she added, "I've been longing to meet you. When I was growing up, I was always desperate to come to Guernsey. I couldn't understand why Mum never took me."

I felt sure that Michele hadn't been brought up in Guernsey but, no longer feeling I was on safe ground, refrained from saying so.

"I think I remember your mum …" I began cautiously, I didn't want to give her false hope and, in any case, the idea was new to me.

"You do?" She gasped.

87

"Well … I remember a young girl coming to live with us one year to help Mum in the guest house."

"Really?!" She sounded thrilled.

"Yes. We shared a room, I remember I loved having her at home with us, and I remember us sitting on the floor and her painting my nails. I'm pretty sure that must have been your Mum."

There was silence on the end of the phone. This meant a lot to her. I waited, not wanting to crowd her, hoping it wasn't all proving too much.

"That's wonderful," she said eventually. And immediately I felt bad because it was such a small offering and she deserved more.

"Maybe she just made regular visits over to see you?" She offered. "It must have been her brother Peter that brought her. He used to be in charge of boats."

"Could be," I said, trying to keep the doubt from my voice. "There's eleven years between us so maybe I was just too young to remember?"

"Would you know of Paimphill or Hinton Martell?" Sharon asked. "They are towns just outside Bournemouth. There's a chalk horse on the hills nearby?" She waited expectantly for my reply, as if certain I would know. And I paused too, sensitive to her feelings but equally certain in my response.

"No, I'm afraid not." How could I be so obtuse? I desperately wanted to help her but couldn't think of anything to say.

"There was a childrens' home in Hinton Martell called St Christopher's? A beautiful old building with a thatched roof? Mum definitely had connections there because she took me and my sisters to visit it several times when we were young. There was a church nearby?"

None of this made any sense to me but still Sharon persevered, convinced she could shake some sort of recollection out of me if she pushed hard enough.

"The home was run by two sisters, Sister Butler and Sister Edenborough? They were nursing sisters. And we met one of mum's friends. A lady called Sally. She had a baby girl?"

Surely I must know?

But still I couldn't help her. None of those clues made any sense to me so I told her, instead, about the German Occupation of Guernsey and how my parents came to be separated for the 5 years of the war. Of how Mum had lived in Bridgwater and Dad had stayed in Guernsey. But I stopped short of saying that Michele could not be my sister because she was so happy to have found me.

If she felt frustrated with me Sharon was kind enough not to show it. Nevertheless, it was time to let someone else try. There was a slight muffling on the other end of the line as the phone exchanged hands.

"Hello Jag, it's Charley here," and before I could respond, "would you remember Michele visiting you in Guernsey in the mid-1990s?"

"Hi Charley, no …"

"… but we have seen pictures from when she was there. Her sister Jackie has blond hair and her daughter is ginger, and I think there was a little boy, too. And there were lots of pictures of Michele with her Dad … "

Charley was talking so fast I could barely catch my breath. Sharon sensed it and took charge, easing it back again, reigning us all in. They were sorry for this intrusion into my life. It must be such a shock. Was I okay? But each time I tried to encourage reason and edge our stories further apart they gently nudged them back together. They had invested too much of themselves in this quest for it not to be true.

Charley had clearly masterminded the project to find me but I was now as eager as she was to try to make sense of the story that underpinned her discovery. There was no denying, however, that we had reached a bit of an impasse. We all had our Sundays to get on with and so, albeit reluctantly, we released each other back to the comfortable familiarity of our separate worlds. For the time being at least, we needed our own space to re-evaluate the past and to work out a new path through the present and on towards our joint future.

The morning had all but disappeared and the buzz of concerted effort to get our BBQ plans back on track proved a welcome distraction. The day was sunny and warm and soon our family had convened on the beach to spend a pleasant afternoon together amongst the sand dunes. We lingered until early evening playing games, swimming and cooking our tea as best we could with the limited resources available.

When at last we got home, tired out from the sunshine, fresh air and the energy of the grandchildren, there was still much work to be done. Food needed to be put away, the dishes washed and I had several lessons to prepare for school the following morning. My subconscious, however, had been hard at work all afternoon and was now ready to present its own agenda for the evening ahead. The first item on the list was to phone my cousin, Val. We had always been close and she was about the same age as Michele so there was a good chance she might remember her. As I picked up the phone I remembered how I had idolised Val as I was growing up. She had always been a constant in my life, more like a sister than a cousin and certainly one of my very best friends.

I can hear my parents busying themselves in their bedroom above, signalling to each other that it is nearly time. I go into the hallway to catch a first glimpse of their glamour. Dad appears first, easy on the stairs, his smile stretching down towards me despite the formality of his suit. He has slicked back his hair to match his shoes, the top and the toe of him, black and shiny. Mum follows, cautiously, her hair swept high onto the top of her head and kept in check by a grid of interlocking kirby grips and several layers of lacquer. She holds lightly onto the bannister as she makes her way daintily down the stairs. With her free hand, she has raised the hem of her long black dress, revealing feet already dressed in sparkly high heels. A fur stole lays lifeless, caressing her shoulders.

The front door opens and in bursts Val, ushering in the cold of winter and the warmth of her fun. I throw myself at her, bombarding her with all that we must do. It will be a long time before she is able to coax me up to bed. They kiss us both and then they are gone. Out into their black, magical night.

Val always looks after me when they go out. We usually spend the night at her house, she has the tiniest bedroom I have ever seen. We snuggle up close and she whispers secrets into my ear for only me to hear. Tonight, for the first time, we are sleeping at my house; I am growing fast and she is ten years older than me, together we have outgrown her single bed.

With a choice of bedrooms, we still choose to sleep together, in the big double bed, in the main front bedroom. The sheets all around us feel damp with the cold but I am warm in her arms. She smells faintly of lavender and there is a hint of smoke on her breath as she swears me to secrecy. We are alone in the house but still she whispers into my ear, as if she is afraid that the walls might hear her.

Our two hearts beat as one as she talks long into the night. She is beautiful, with raven hair and deep brown eyes, but I love her more because she is exciting and funny. She laughs and plays games with me and she comes to see me every day on her way *home from school.*

Of her many admirers, she is asking, which should she choose? But I am close to sleep now and so I leave her secrets to fill my heart to bursting so proud am I that she should choose to confide in me.

"Hello! It's me!"

"Hi Jack, everything okay?" she sounded concerned. It was unusual for me to call her at this time on a Sunday evening.

"Yeah fine. I've got some really exciting news …"

Bypassing all pleasantries I launched straight into my story, tripping over details that were as yet unfamiliar to me. I hadn't got far when the depth of her silence started slowing me down before rapidly pulling me to a complete stop. Val, one of my most special people, was not sharing the excitement of this particular journey in the way I had expected she would. And the reason was simple … she already knew its destination.

"Yes, Jackie." She sighed and then paused, as if buying herself time. "You do have a sister and her name is Michele."

For a long while, neither of us spoke. It was hard, from both our perspectives, to find the right words to cut through the silence. Did she feel guilty? Frightened of my reaction maybe? Or had she simply never thought to prepare herself for the day that I might find out? The safe, secure, world of her was starting to crumble and she knew it. It was up to her now.

"When your mum was in England during the war she had a baby," she began cautiously, feeling her way as if she were steering through dangerous currents that might easily sweep us away. I waited silently for her to gain the courage to continue. "But when the war ended, as you know, she came back here to your dad. She couldn't bring the baby with her, it would have been too scandalous, so she left her in the UK. It was a girl, and her name was Michele. My mum told me …"

She paused again, determined this time to wait for my reaction, but I was too shocked to speak.

"Your mum and dad paid for Michele to be brought up in a home." She continued eventually, knowing that she owed it to me to tell me the truth. " I was sixteen when she came over here to live with you, so you must have been six. I remember her well but you were probably too young to remember much? She came to help your mum in the guest house, and she did for a while but …"

This time I didn't hold back. "But what?"

"Well, they started arguing. And eventually, she ran away. I'm pretty sure I have a picture somewhere of her sitting on a wall …"

"Why did you never tell me?" I asked, struggling to keep my voice neutral.

"When I'm told a secret, Jackie, I never tell anyone!"

I thought beyond the secrets that Val had made me swear not to tell anyone to this one secret she had held from me for fifty years. It was a secret that rightfully belonged to me and should not have been hers to keep. I could find no words.

Persuaded by the depth of my silence, she softened her tone. "My mum did once say that she thought you ought to be told. I think it was when your dad died. But I told her it wasn't the right time …"

"What happened to her after she ran away?"

"I have no idea. I never heard anyone speak about her after she left."

The details she had given were disappointingly sketchy, perhaps because her many protestations were genuine and this was all that she could remember, or perhaps because she still chose to hold on to some part of it. Either way, she had told me just about enough to satisfy the moment. I sensed anticipation as we both fell silent, but she had no need to worry, my heart would never lose its love for her and my spirit would always perhaps be a little over-generous. And when I finally let her go, albeit a little earlier than she deserved, we both knew that any reprieve was likely to be temporary.

I sat, quietly alone, for a long time after replacing the receiver. The outcome of the phone call had not been at all what I had been expecting. Upstairs Charlie was playing his guitar, and in the kitchen, Pete was clearing away the dishes, but this was certainly not a normal Sunday evening in our household. My world had paused, as if awaiting instruction as to how to proceed. And those around me were waiting too, quietly gauging my reaction and readying their support for when I should need it. Suddenly my thoughts turned to my father, just as they always seemed to when I needed reassurance.

He is sitting, his slim frame at ease in his armchair, and I am standing close beside him. We are in our lounge at Romo and I am six years old. I am dressed simply in white ankle socks, a red and black checked dress and a Guernsey jumper that is slightly too small. He is leaning forwards so our heads are touching, his arm around my waist, holding me close to comfort me.

"Where is she, Daddy?"

Dad pulls a white handkerchief from his pocket, it feels soft and silky smooth on my cheek as he wipes away the tears. In the kitchen, Mum is busying herself tidying away the dishes. There is a loud crash, the sound of a saucepan falling onto a hard floor. She is uncharacteristically careless today.

"We didn't know where she was last night darling. We think she may have a boyfriend. Your mum is very upset, but you mustn't

let it worry you, everything will work out okay in the end."

And then Michele is running, to the top of the hill and beyond, as fast as she can away from us. Our family is broken, and my dad is sitting on my bed in my winter bedroom calming my distress.

What a day it had been! I felt as though I had been catapulted, out of my orderly and predictable macro world, into some strange quantum existence in which anything was possible and nothing made sense. Nevertheless, as random thoughts continued to play hide and seek with my powers of reason, I could feel parts of the past unlocking.

I remembered the excitement and anticipation of her arrival; the love and the hope. Enough ingredients, surely, to secure a happy ending? Except it all depended on the bond between mother and daughter. A bond established too late in life for either of them to have confidence in its reality. When freedom beckoned Michele she ran to it, through the lanes at the top of the hill and towards a life in exile that was surely not in any of our best interests.

In the midst of all this turmoil, one person had waited long enough. I had loved her once yet somehow had lost even the memory of her. I knew precisely what I must do. Without hesitation, I picked up my pen.

21st June 2009

Dear Michele,

I can only imagine how you must be feeling now and how you must have felt in the past. The happiness that I feel learning that you are my sister is tinged with so much pain and regret. Please know that I long to speak with you and to meet you – I long to meet your family – and for you to meet mine. I am so very sorry for everything (not my fault I know) but I am so very sorry. Please call me if you feel you can when you feel ready. We can just talk about the weather if you like – anything to just make contact – a start. You can call me anytime day or night – I will be so pleased to hear from you.

Sending you all my love.

Your sister,

Jackie

xx

CHAPTER 4

Michele

MONDAY 22ND JUNE 2009

Hi Jag,

Mum was well shocked when I told her I spoke with you. She did not know that you never knew of her which makes us all very sad. Mum is only too pleased to scan photos for you. I don't know what thoughts are going around in her head. Mum also said she will, of course, speak to you. I am sure between you both you can shed some light.

Thank you again,
Sharon

It had only been a week since that first email from Charley, but in that week my whole world had changed. With so much to distract me from my working day, I found myself continually popping home during lunchtimes or extended free periods, just in case there was any new information for me or the chance for a quick chat with either my new niece or great-niece. We had more than enough willing participants on each side of the English Channel to make sense of everything, or so we imagined, and, in those early days after the discovery of my new family, I had daily contact with them. It had taken many years for their detective work to reach fruition so they were always pleased to hear from me, but their hope was for answers that were not mine to give.

Michele didn't reply to my letter, nor did she acknowledge receipt of it through her daughter or granddaughter. Perhaps she kept it from them, hidden away in the safety of her private thoughts, placed inside a cache of other secrets that she would never open for anyone. She was the leading lady in our drama, yet she refused to even take to the stage. So it was entirely down to Sharon, Charley and me to try to make sense of the past. We moved forwards cautiously, mindful of every twist and turn that might challenge our loyalties, whilst united in our mission to uncover the truth. As we opened our hearts and gifted our clues, small parts of the story did occasionally start to fit together. But mostly we just succeeded in generating further questions; questions that played hide and seek with our minds and tug-of-war with our powers of reason.

One such question that weighed particularly heavily on my mind, was the identity of the Jacqueline Le Bargy who had been born in Newton Abbott on the 12th November 1942; the Jacqueline Le Bargy they had originally believed to be me. For my part, I was beginning to believe that anything might be possible so it was with considerable relief that I was able to locate, and present to them, a copy of my birth certificate verifying my birth in Guernsey in 1956. So who was this other Jacqueline Le Bargy?

Then there was Michele's brother Peter? They were clear that he was not to be confused with her brother-in-law (and my husband) Peter. Nor was it possible that he was baby Michael who had passed away.

"Mum said he was a handyman of sorts," Sharon told me. "I always imagined him in white overalls with a tools pouch around his waist."

"Nan told me he was a motor mechanic," Charley added. "I think he may have worked in a garage and he definitely had a strong connection with boats."

None of this made any sense to me and, when I asked Val, she couldn't remember a single person called Peter or indeed anyone that might fit this description.

I was also fascinated by the photos that Sharon and Charley had talked about in our first phone call and I enquired after them many times. Sharon's response was always the same.

"Mum came round one day and asked if she could borrow some family photos to take to show her dad in Guernsey. He was poorly, apparently, and she wanted to see him. I didn't think anything of it at the time. She often spoke about him …."

"When exactly was this?"

"Mid-1990s I think. When Mum returned from Guernsey she brought back photos of her dad, her sister Jackie and her niece that she had taken during the visit."

"I'd really love to see those photos," I said, each time trying not to sound too pushy.

"Of course! We'll scan them and send them to you as soon as we find them."

It was frustrating that Sharon wasn't sure where the photos were, but it was clear that both she and Charley had studied them carefully in the past because they were able to accurately recall and describe the people they featured. There could be no doubt as to whom they were referring. I felt sure these photos would answer a lot of my questions; I just needed to see them. But I still had no recollection of meeting anyone in the mid-1990s that could possibly have been Michele and, as time went on and the photos didn't materialise, I began to wonder if they really did exist. With so many other lines of enquiry pulling us in different directions I was reluctant to put further pressure on Sharon and Charley to find them and so, eventually, I stopped asking.

Although I loved to talk with Sharon and Charley, I felt

increasingly uneasy that Michele was showing no interest in their quest to find me, and I was anxious as to what this might mean for our future. What if she didn't want anything to do with me? I would have to respect her right to privacy. My life felt as if it had been placed on hold. Pete was frustrated too. He had been at my side from the start, and remained deeply touched by the emotional journey that this represented for so many people. But he was also a practical man, a problem solver, and not afraid to take control of a situation if he felt it justified.

"Why don't you just ask Sharon for Michele's number and phone her?!"

And sometimes his frustration threatened to overcome my resolve. However, in my heart, I knew I must wait until the time was right. The first move had to come from her.

In the end, she phoned me when I was least expecting it and when I had all but given up hope of hearing from her. Her voice sounded strange and her accent strong, just as mine must have sounded to her, and she talked so quickly it was hard to keep pace with her words. My heart raced with anticipation and the sudden, irrational fear that we might find we had nothing to say to each other. Unprepared, I stumbled awkwardly through a few pleasantries before finding common ground in our love of dogs. She owned a chocolate Labrador called Coco with whom she was besotted and I told her about our new black Labrador puppy, Mali. The neutrality of the conversation calmed both our nerves and before long we were both perfectly at ease.

"What's the weather like back home then?" she asked.

"It's been lovely here the past few days," I replied, hoping I had hidden my surprise at her reference to Guernsey as her home. "What's your weather like?"

"Lovely," she pronounced it as if it was two words.

"Mummy and Daddy loved it on the beach when it was hot

didn't they? Daddy used to drive us in the car." She said it so naturally that I was momentarily taken aback. Having been raised as an only child this narrative was alien to me, but I also found it deeply comforting. And, however much I craved answers, I didn't push her for more than she was willing to give. We were on the road again, our journey back on track, and I knew that, wherever it led, I would be there for the duration.

One thing was certain, I couldn't wait any longer, I needed to meet her; to see her with my own eyes; to talk with her and to walk alongside her. I was also longing to meet Sharon and Charley. On the spur of the moment, Pete and I decided that we would go to London the following weekend. My nieces were delighted, they were sure Michele would feel the same. I was not so certain, but they were the ones who knew her best and all I could do was hope that they were right. I booked the plane tickets, booked somewhere to stay and before long we found ourselves booking into the hotel.

I had been far too preoccupied over the previous few days to consider the logistics of our visit. I had chosen the hotel for its proximity to my new family; close but not too close. I hadn't realised that it lay right in the middle of the business district. High tower blocks and sterile streets surrounded us and the hotel felt dark and gloomy. Our room was equally uninspiring. Squashed under the eaves at the back of the building it felt angular and awkward. Overloaded with dark, heavy furniture, it might have totally defeated me had it not been for the beautiful flower arrangement from Sharon and Charley that greeted our arrival. I phoned Sharon to thank her and to arrange where we might meet. Neither of us had any idea what sort of place the other might like so we decided to meet at our hotel at 7pm.

The intervening hours proved an enormous challenge. There would have been enough time to venture out and explore a more agreeable area of London, but neither Pete nor I could summon up the appetite for that. Given the enormity of the moment that lay ahead of us, it seemed wisest to rest up and relax while we could. For me, this proved a big mistake.

The slowing of time fired up my inner turmoil and before long it was wreaking havoc on my nerves. I found it impossible to settle to anything. I paced the floor of the tiny room wondering if I was doing the right thing. What would my mother have thought of it all? Would she have been pleased I was meeting my sister at last? I somehow doubted it. And the question, that had been burning in my heart since the first contact with my new family, continued to torment me. In reaching out and making this connection with them was I being disloyal to her?

When it was finally time to go down to the hotel lobby I felt sick with excitement and dread. What if I had completely misjudged the timing and it was too soon to meet? But Pete reminded me that there was nothing to be gained by questioning wheels that had already been set in motion. We just needed to do everything in our power to ensure that they took us in the right direction.

We waited in the hotel lobby until well past the appointed hour and, by the time they emerged from the back of a black London cab, I had become so highly sprung that I swooped upon them leaving Sharon and Charley momentarily shocked. I don't think they had expected me to be so tall. But they greeted me warmly and I instantly felt I had known them forever. Standing a few paces behind them, looking anxious and slightly lost, was my mother. Or at least a woman whose resemblance to her took my breath away. I had lost Mum 21 years earlier yet here were her features before me again; her stature and her genes in her daughter Michele. It felt wonderful to see her living on in someone else after all this time. It was a second chance of sorts and one I was determined to embrace. I hugged Michele and she hugged me back, it seemed that she would give it a go; it was all I could expect.

We ate together in the hotel that first night. It was posher than any of us felt comfortable with but time was precious and, though we had wandered the neighbourhood for a short while, we hadn't been able to find anywhere more suitable close by. A chaos of emotion surrounded us, binding us together whilst holding us apart. We wanted to tell the world of our fortune but instead, we told only our waitress as we filled our cameras with photos and our hearts with each other.

As we sat and talked I became mesmerised by Sharon. Never had I seen the pain of empathy worn so openly on anyone's face. Understated and self-deprecating, she wore a simple black dress that allowed her natural beauty to shine through. She was a magnificent storyteller, delightfully funny yet never unkind, the sort of person that always sees the good in people and brings the best out of everyone simply by being herself. Charley was equally funny but in a fast and feisty way. She was an attractive girl, with a clever wit and a lightning mind that were constantly tripping over each other in their race to be first. It was she, as I had guessed, who had masterminded most of the research to date and I looked forward to some time alone with her to pick her brains.

As the conversation danced to and fro between us, Michele held herself quietly back and observed us from the shadows. She seemed reluctant to join in the game, as her daughter and granddaughter searched for the similarities in our looks, our mannerisms and the way we were. It was an evening that I wanted to last forever, yet one that I couldn't wait to look back on. When it finally came to an end, we hugged each other tightly before they climbed into the cab that would take them back to their lives in South East London. Pete and I waved them off and then retired to our room. But it was impossible to sleep. Instead, we talked long into the early hours of the next morning, reliving every moment of our extraordinary evening. And, as I finally started to drift off to sleep, I wondered what their conversation must have been like, in the back of the black cab on their way home that night.

By mid-morning we were ready to go again and we set off to meet them for a river cruise. They had arrived before us, already taking charge of the tickets and our passage onto the boat. Three generations of the same family and each of them excited to meet with us again. With so much along the banks of the Thames to entertain us, the conversation flowed as easily as the river, but my real interest lay in the way the three of them interacted with each other and with those all around them. It was fascinating to watch as each perfectly complemented the other two to act as one united team. They were friendly and helpful to everyone they encountered, full of cheerful banter, and always standing ready to assist or to scold according to need.

We stopped at Greenwich for a stroll and, as we sat in the café waiting for our lunch, I gave them the few carefully chosen mementoes that I had brought from home.

"This is a Red Cross letter that Mum sent to Dad during the war," I said passing the fragile sheet of paper to Sharon who took it gratefully. "They were only allowed to send 25 words to each other, and no more than once a month."

It was a gentle reminder that my parents had been separated by the war. Sharon's eyes clouded a little as she embraced the nostalgia that this letter represented. She raised it gently to brush it past her lips before passing it on to Charley.

"And here is a photo of Mum holding Anneka when she was a baby."

I watched Sharon closely, to see if she saw in the image what I saw. Anneka was six months old and looking cheekily into the camera whilst Mum was looking straight past her and into the distance. Wistful. As if she were searching out some great sadness that lay on the horizon.

"I wonder what she must have been thinking?" whispered Sharon.

Michele had forgotten to bring the photos that I had been hoping to see but I hid my disappointment. She would show them to me when she was ready.

As our second day drew to a close and we went our separate ways I felt privileged to have been included, if only for a short while, as part of their team. Our lives were, in every way different, but the bond between us felt comfortable and strong. Back at the hotel I finally allowed myself to relax as Pete and I shared our thoughts over a bottle of wine and some tapas. It all seemed to be going well and I felt giddy with happiness. Sleep would come much more easily that night.

On our third and final day, Sharon and Charley decided to leave us to it and Michele turned up, instead, with her partner Martin. We enjoyed a drink together in a riverside pub and we laughed as she tugged, playfully on my scarf whilst Pete tried to take a photo. After a stroll along the banks of the Thames, they treated us to a roast dinner in a converted barn nearby. As we sat waiting for our meal to arrive, Michele started to assume the role of big sister.

"We're in London now Bubba. Not Guernsey. Folks will take that bag if you don't hang onto it," she scolded.

"Put your cardigan on Bubba. You don't want to catch a chill."

She was becoming easy in my company and I was glad of it. Best of all she told me she had brought the photos and I could barely contain my excitement at the clues they might hold. Still, I needed to be patient. It was not until the meal was cleared away and we sat back in our seats to relax over coffee that she decided it was time to reach into her handbag.

The first item she passed me was a gift bag from Sharon containing a silver-framed group photograph taken on our boat journey the day before. I took a few moments to appreciate this thoughtful gesture. It was certainly a photograph that I knew I would always treasure. Then, finally, she withdrew from her bag a small clutch of prints. I held my breath as she carefully started shuffling through them, searching, almost furtively for what she should offer me first.

"There you go girl!" she said with a flourish, handing me the first of her treasures.

I recognised the photograph immediately. Mum, Anneka and myself, taken in my parents' back garden during the summer of 1988. Mum looked really well though it was barely two months before she died. I thought back to that afternoon, my parents had been looking after Anneka whilst I was at school. The day was sunny and warm, we had enjoyed a cup of tea and a chat in the garden, and then Dad had got out his camera to take a few shots. There were some lovely group portraits, the last ones ever taken with Mum. Judging by the handful of prints Michele held close to her chest she must have a copy of each of them.

So their timescale was wrong? This was definitely taken in the late 1980s. Perhaps I had been right after all and I hadn't met Michele in the mid-1990s? Perhaps Dad had simply posted these photos to her? But why would he have done that? He had always looked out for me and it seemed oddly out of character that he should give these photos to her without mentioning anything to me, especially since they would have enabled her to come and find me after his death. Is that what he wanted? And why, then, would Michele have told Sharon, in the mid-1990s, that she had visited him?

Questions and more questions. Always.

I had my own copies of all the photographs so I knew them well, but I prepared to share Michele's delight in them, they meant a lot to her and I needed to be sensitive to that. She hesitated before passing me the second photo. As if she were slightly reluctant to let it go. And she watched closely for my reaction as I took it. As soon as I saw the image I realised I had been mistaken, this photo was from a completely different batch than the first one and I had never seen it before.

I studied the two people sitting side by side on a sofa. His sofa! They were leaning slightly apart and looking at each other as they laughed, eyes shining with joy. Beside them was a box of chocolates and a bottle of whisky. I was deeply touched by the happiness in the image and the smile that I gave her was genuine. Returning my smile, and looking slightly relieved, she handed me the remaining photos.

I took them from her gently, lingering over the images, taking time to absorb their content and process their meaning. The same two protagonists were in each, sharing chocolates and toasting each other's good health with tumblers full of whiskey. There was such warmth and love in the photos and the hint of a reunion that had been too long in the making.

When I reached the last of the photos, the lump in my throat hardened. I took a deep breath, hoping she hadn't sensed it, and tried to steady the rush of thoughts that threatened to derail me. I had never seen the photo before, but the narrative behind it was clear. It was the autumn of 1995 and the two of them were standing on his doorstep, hugging each other tightly, reluctant to let each other go. Dad and Michele, father and daughter, their eyes shining with emotion, were saying goodbye to each other for the very last time. I blinked away the tears and handed my sister's precious bundle of photos back to her with a watery smile.

CHAPTER 5

A New Era

AT FIFTY-THREE YEARS OLD life had finally delivered me the sister that I had not only longed for, but had subconsciously half expected to find. With every step I took forwards with her, however, I took a step backwards into the past to try to discover the truth that lay beneath our wings. To my shame and subsequent regret, I had not only shown little interest in my parents' wartime experiences, I had never shown any real interest in their actual lives, or in any matter relating to our collective past. All that changed when I first lifted the phone to speak to my new family, but by then it was too late.

As different lines of enquiry opened up in front of me I flitted from one to another searching for the big breakthrough that would answer all my questions. Instead, each one led me, in turn, down blind alleys or towards dead ends and I soon realised that, if I did not take more care, the task ahead would completely overwhelm me. Many times I had to step back from the pull of the search to allow myself time to heal.

Losing my mother so suddenly had made me more appreciative of my father in the final few years of his life and meant that I was more mindful of making the most of the time that I had left with him. It was hard to see him left alone after Mum passed but he never made our daily interactions more difficult than they needed to be. My father was a contented soul with an unfaltering pride that assumed, without question, that his side of the fence was always the greenest. I admired this outlook, he lived life according to his means and never complained, despite being held hostage many times by his failing health.

In later life, when old age had stolen his breath and confined him to the most sedentary of lifestyles, he would watch the world go by from his seat near the window, and so live vicariously through the comings and goings of his fellow islanders. This was the pre-digital age, but I often imagine, had he been given a few more years, how he might have embraced the wonders of the internet. He could have shopped online and travelled the world from the comfort of his armchair, long after his fragile health had confined him to the indoors. And he would have shared a drink, as I now do in his place, with our relatives in Australia on Skype. Knowing my father, he would have made the most of every minute.

My parents were fiercely proud of the many changes they had seen during their extraordinary lifetimes but, with the internet, would come possibilities that they could never have imagined. Their stoic generation could have had no concept of the lightning speed of change that the digital revolution would issue in, or how the trail of their past could so sharply be brought back into focus. Grief had failed to break their generation and, though they had kow-towed to the moral pressures of the time, they had always been in control of what others knew about them. They had lived out their lives secure in the knowledge that their past remained protected from even the most prying of eyes. It was a strategy that had worked well for decades. But times had changed. Much of their past lay directly underneath my fingertips, I just needed to develop the skills necessary to access it.

As a matter of priority I became a fully paid-up member of Ancestry.com and barely stopped to draw breath as I began my own journey back into the archives of our past. It was quick and easy to navigate through the vast data files of family history and it wasn't long before I had mastered enough basic research techniques to find her:

BIRTHS REGISTERED IN JANUARY, FEBRUARY, MARCH 1945

	Mother's maiden name	District
Le Bargy, Michele	Loveridge	Bournemouth

Further proof, had I needed it, that Michele was my half-sister, born during the war while my mother was living in Bridgwater. I paused to reflect on the personal tragedy that this represented for so many people. The search engines did not, however, find Jacqueline Le Bargy but they did find a record that came close:

BIRTHS REGISTERED IN OCTOBER, NOVEMBER, DECEMBER 1942

	Mother's maiden name	District
Le Bargy, (Female)	Loveridge	Newton A.

"That's amazing news," Sharon said excitedly when I rang to tell her. "But I have definitely seen her called Jacqueline."

"Well, it only says female on Ancestry," I said, certain that there was no Jacqueline Le Bargy to be found in the English records.

"Charley and I went up to the registry office at Kew and I took a photo of the registration," Sharon replied, equally sure. "It definitely said Jacqueline."

"Do you still have the photo?" I asked hopefully.

"It was on an old phone ... I think I've lost it."

I guessed that Michele had spoken so often of her sister Jacqueline that they had conflated this with the birth entry at Kew. But I knew I would never convince them of this and it didn't really matter. I had found the entry they had referred to, I just needed to try to make sense of it. The next person I phoned was Val, but this time she couldn't help me. She knew nothing of a second baby and felt sure that Auntie Dink had known nothing too. I had no particular reason to doubt her and, in any case, I believed I had already worked out the most plausible explanation for myself.

It is early February 1994 and I am sitting in my father's lounge. I have just left the hospital and the pain in the room is palpable. Dad and I are struggling to find the dialogue to cut through it. I lost her yesterday, four months into a wretched pregnancy and after finally being given the go-ahead to get up from bedrest and carry on with life. Dad will understand I know, because he lost a baby too; my brother, Michael. Michael would have been in his mid-fifties now; if only he had lived.

"Try not to worry, darling," he ventures, "everything will work out in the end. It always does."

"But I'm 37, Dad," I say, beginning to articulate my innermost fear. "I might not be able to conceive again. Remember the difficulty Mum had after she lost Michael?"

She had told me this, I was certain. Even if she hadn't, with 16 years between Michael and me there must have been something wrong.

"Why would you think she had a problem?!" he asks sharply, and with an edge to his voice that I have never heard before. It shocks me into silence. But he has started and he knows he must continue.

"Mum was pregnant when she evacuated … the baby girl she was carrying was stillborn in the UK at eight months."

He blurts the words out in a manner so uncharacteristic of my father that I am too overcome with emotion to respond. Instead, I

*write them carefully in my heart, so that I might ponder over, and
mourn them, another day.*

If Mum had been pregnant when she evacuated then this
registry of birth must be the baby girl that she had delivered
stillborn in the UK. Admittedly the date was wrong, the baby
girl would have been stillborn in November 1940 not 1942 but I
felt sure that could be explained by a simple transcription error.
A zero could easily pass as a two if it had been hastily inscribed.
And this 1940s typo must simply have passed unchallenged
down the generations and become accepted as fact. War
records were notoriously inaccurate. I was sure I had read that
somewhere?

This second tragedy had befallen Mum just a few months
after losing Michael; it was heartbreaking. With determination,
I set about trying to prove my theory. I phoned the registry
office in Newton Abbott, briefly explained my quest and was
put through to a kindly sounding lady who asked for a few
more details before delivering her verdict.

"Miscarriages and stillbirths are recorded in a private
register," she explained. "If you could prove you were a blood
relation you would have the right to request the information.
But it's doubtful as to whether that sort of information will
have survived I'm afraid. Those kind of records were often lost
during the war."

"But there is a definite record of her birth," I countered. "I've
seen it. The surnames are too unusual for it to be anyone other
than my mother."

The lady paused for a moment. Deliberating. Not wanting to
give me false hope.

"Well," she said finally, "maybe the baby lived for a brief

period after delivery? In that case, the birth would have been recorded, but then there would be a record of her death. So you could try searching for that?"

I had already partially pursued that line of enquiry, but deaths required a far more proactive and detailed online search than births and I had to admit that I had been rather half-hearted in my initial search. So I decided to try again, and sat long into the night, systematically trawling through all the records of deaths around that time. Still, I found nothing.

I awoke the next morning feeling strangely energised. I had been living on adrenalin since this new direction had taken hold of my life and it was still very exciting. For years I had maintained a delicate balancing act between a job that was intense and demanding, and raising my family. Any personal satisfaction that I sought from life had been almost exclusively derived through them. There hadn't been time for anything else. My children were older now, and no longer needed me with the same immediacy they once had and that was sometimes hard to accept. The discovery of my new family had come at just the right time. It was giving me a whole new focus and had put me right at the centre of my life again. It felt good.

With so much laying beneath my fingertips I found it surprisingly difficult to accept that some information is simply not available online. When the computer stubbornly refused to shed any further light on the matter of this Le Bargy baby I picked up the telephone again. The lady was pleased to hear that I had followed her advice but was at a loss as to what to suggest next.

"You could always order her birth certificate?" she offered finally and somewhat tentatively.

"How would that help?" I wasn't convinced. "Surely it would simply confirm the information I've already found online?"

"You would be surprised," she said gaining conviction. "I've known of several cases where there has been extra information written in the margins. I don't think you really have any other option do you?"

Frustrated and disappointed at the brick wall I had come up against, I went online for the last time that day to order her birth certificate. I had no idea how this could possibly help me, but I had been persuaded that it was at least worth a try. The decision would give me partial closure on this particular line of enquiry, for the time being at least, and enable me to focus on Michele and her family.

I had almost forgotten I had sent for it when the correspondence finally arrived from the General Registry Office and I had no expectation that it would further my cause. Nevertheless, as I slid the copy of her birth certificate out of its tightly fitting envelope, I felt the thrill of a baby's life as she suddenly became real.

She was born on the 12th November 1942 at Hazelwood Nursing Home, Lower Warberry Road, Torquay. Her mother was Kathleen Adele Le Bargy, formerly Loveridge, a butcher's cashier of 31 High Street, Bridgwater. The column for her father's name remained blank as I had expected, but then my eye was drawn to the right-hand margin where, carefully inscribed and underlined in black ink, was a single word ... <u>Adopted</u>.

CHAPTER 6

I Know You're Out There Somewhere

NEVER HAD A SINGLE word held so much power over me. Time after time I pulled the piece of paper from its envelope and studied its contents, wondering if I had misinterpreted it, certain I must have missed something. Even with the evidence in my hand, my conviction struggled to back down, admit defeat and let go of the persuasive logic. I had been so certain that this baby was the stillbirth that Dad had told me about that I had failed to consider any other possibility. But each time I looked in the margins at the word, my sister became more and more alive ... <u>Adopted</u>.

A kaleidoscope of colour streams through the stained glass window at Romo, painting Mum's hair with its magic and dancing on the walls behind her. She is standing motionless in the hallway below me as I look down on her from the middle stair, a single frame from the movie of our lives.

She is reading a letter; a significant letter. And for some reason, that I cannot quite reach, she is explaining the meaning of adoption. She emphasises the finality; there can be no going back. She tells me to quell my questions, but I cannot let them rest, I am sure that there must be a way.

"I am too old now to have more children," she answers me finally, swallowing the tears as she shuts down my dreams.

And I know I must not ask again because it is the first time I have seen her cry and the lack of hope in her voice has unsettled me.

Once again I phoned Val, but she genuinely seemed to have no more idea about this second baby than I had. Then I phoned Sharon and Charley. They were as excited as I was at this unexpected news and we all agreed that this was definitely the person they had originally thought was me. Their research had uncovered three sisters rather than two. They asked if I would be willing to send for Michele's birth certificate also, in case it provided similar detail. Of course, I wanted to do as much as I could to help them but I felt uncomfortable with this particular request. Michele and I were in regular contact now, speaking often on the phone, carefully and respectfully dodging awkward questions. I still sensed it was "out of bounds" to talk about her past in any meaningful way. And, though I would always remain desperate for answers, what we had was far more important to me than making sense of the past. She had been deeply hurt in ways that I could only imagine and I recognised the need to always be sensitive to that. This was her story not mine and I didn't want to do anything that might upset her. After much soul-searching, however, I agreed to the request. There was no doubt that Sharon and Charley had Michele's best interests at heart; it wasn't for me to question their wishes. So I did as they requested and ordered Michele's birth certificate.

Great expectation accompanied the wait for the paperwork which turned to disappointment soon after it arrived. The certificate informed us that Michele Le Bargy had been born on 15th January 1945 at 23 Knole Road, Bournemouth. Her mother's name was Kathleen Adele Le Bargy, formerly Loveridge, of 11 Kidsbury Road, Bridgwater. As expected, there was no mention of the baby's father and the margins were empty.

Meanwhile, I had once again turned my back on sleep. I would rest when I had found my adopted sister. Too much of our lives had played out already and each of us had only so many grains of sand remaining. There must be evidence of her somewhere on the world wide web, if I could just find out where to look. But I quickly learnt that all search engines are on the side of the adopted, protecting their privacy and leaving them to live their lives in complete anonymity, if that is how they wished it. There were tantalising glimpses of them, lying safely hidden behind a seemingly impermeable membrane. They could reach through it to me, if they wanted, but I would need to secure their permission to reach back to them in return. It hardly seemed fair to be tormented in this way, and I gave too much of myself to this cruel and compulsive game. A game that would throw me the occasional glimmer of hope before casting me adrift, further from the truth than when I had started.

It was hard to accept that social constraints could still hold such power over me. Before a change in the adoption laws, that came into effect at the very end of 2005, I would not even have had the right to try to find her. As it was, I was forced to accept the fact that the internet was unable to deliver her to me. My only hope, and indeed my only right, was to approach her through an intermediary agency that would carry out the search on my behalf.

During the spring of 2010, I made contact with AAA NORCAP, a charity set up to help adults affected by adoption. Their mission, for a substantial fee, was to trace my sister and guide me through the process of bringing us together if, of course, this was acceptable to her. They were kind and sympathetic in their dealings with me, yet meticulous in their care not to give false hope. There would be no shortcuts on this particular journey. Where it might lead no one dared predict, to a dead-end quite possibly, or worse still, to a door that was firmly locked against me. Were they fortunate enough to find her, it would be she alone who would determine the outcome. I signed my acceptance, paid the initial fee up front and sat back and waited. It was not long before I received some initial news.

23rd May 2010

Dear Jacqueline,

I am pleased to inform you that the first stage of the process is now complete for the Birth Relative Intermediary Service. If you would like to call the office we will be able to update you on the progress so far and also discuss with you everything you can remember or know about the birth and adoption as this can sometimes assist us to provide you with a speedier service.

We look forward to talking with you,

Service Team Leader

The letter had been written on my birthday and I considered that a good sign. I phoned the office immediately and a sympathetic voice told me that they had found out her name, which regrettably could not yet be shared with me, and that they would now begin to research her marital status and whether she was currently registered with a doctor in the UK. It was good news I was sure, but I could find no way of processing this information or determining how I should feel. All my questions were off-limits and I had no power over progress. The phone call had been brief but the wait would now be long.

On the tenth of August impatience got the better of me and I phoned for an update. There was news and it was encouraging. She was currently registered with a doctor somewhere in England or Wales and she was married. My heart danced at the implication that my sister was alive and living in the UK, but the joy was short-lived. They had not yet discovered whether she had placed a veto on contact from her birth family. Adoption could still be irrevocable even after all these years.

Later that summer I received further news, there was no veto. Furthermore:

I hope you will be pleased to hear that we have located your sister and will be moving to the intermediary stage once we have established whether we can locate her adoption file.

In an instant, she had become a reality, almost close enough for me to touch. I didn't dare ask what would happen if they were unable to locate her adoption file. I simply paid the extra money they requested to enable them to continue with their enquiries and prepared for another long wait.

As Christmas approached I received a call from a lady called Patricia. We had spoken a few months previously, when I had tried to circumvent the official channels in the stubborn conviction that I could find my sister myself. She had respectfully pointed me towards AAA NORCAP and was now contacting me on their behalf, as an intermediary to guide me through the final stages of the process. We arranged for her to visit.

I liked Patricia immediately. She was tall and slim, with greying hair and a casual formality to her dress that suggested a no-nonsense approach to life. As I welcomed her into my home I felt the weight lift from my shoulders. Here was someone who could offer the professional help that I so desperately needed; a travelling companion for the last leg of my journey.

"I'm sorry I wasn't in a position to help you when you first phoned me," she said as we both sat down. "I'm afraid it's necessary to go through all the formal channels first."

"It's me who should apologise for trying to short-cut the process," I said, realising that I must have put her in a difficult position.

"No problem. I was at least able to point you in the right direction and now here we are!"

"Yes!"

Patricia sat bolt upright on the edge of her seat with her hands clasped firmly in her lap. She had angled her body so that she could look directly at me. Her eyes danced with excitement.

"As I told you on the phone we have managed to obtain contact details for your adopted sister!"

"It's so exciting!" I said, barely able to control my emotions. There was excitement, yes, but caution too …

"And I am here to help you think about your next step. To help you decide whether you want to go ahead and try to make contact with her. It's a big decision and you shouldn't rush it."

The chronology made little sense to me. I had already invested heavily in the quest to find my sister, both financially and emotionally. Of course, I wanted to make contact. But I was no expert and it was clear that Patricia wanted to ensure the best possible outcome for all concerned so I needed to be careful to keep to her script.

"Why don't you start by telling me the story so far," she suggested, relaxing back in her chair, as if trying to calm me down. And I needed little encouragement to take centre stage because it was a story that was precious to me and one that I enjoyed telling to a receptive audience.

So I relaxed back in my chair, too, and began with Charley's first email and the sense it had evoked of a mystery that lingered somewhere in my past. I told her of Michele's initial reticence, of our first meeting, of the photos of her and my dad and of the path that led to the discovery of three sisters rather than two. And when I finished she could see that I had trodden much of this path before.

Skilfully and gently she questioned me, encouraging me to dig deeper, to confront the issues that I found most worrying. It wasn't long before she had me voicing my innermost fears:

"What if we make contact and she doesn't even know she's adopted?"

"What if we choose a really bad time to approach her?"

"What if this all ends in tears (hers and mine)?"

It was a relief to open up to Patricia in this way and, though she didn't have the power to address all of my concerns, she was able to offer reassurance for the one question that was uppermost in my mind.

"Do you think I am doing the right thing in trying to make contact with her?"

And I trusted her answer, which was a cautious yet unequivocal "Yes!" because the sensitivity with which Patricia was handling my situation, and the empathy she showed for both my mother and my sister, had been evident from the start. Our life stories felt safe in her hands.

We agreed to reconvene early in the New Year once Christmas, and its power to emotionally unhinge all but the most vigilant had passed. In the meantime, as Patricia had requested, I reached into my soul to examine my motives and to confirm that I really did want to make contact with my adopted sister.

And so, as I enjoyed the festive period with my family and friends, I wondered … was I just being selfish? Was I being disloyal to Mum? If this emotional investment left me bankrupt could I pick myself up? Could I live the rest of my life knowing that I had paid the price for others to discover what I had lost?

Yet surely someone would fight my corner! Give testimony to my good qualities and gently nudge her path towards mine. I had forgotten that there could be no coercion or even the slightest hint of persuasion. Indeed, no pressure of any kind would ever be placed upon her. She was the judge and she was the jury and if I thought that even the tiniest part of me would be able to reach out to influence her decision I was very much mistaken.

CHAPTER 7

The Game of Patience

IT WAS A COLD, dark evening in early January 2011 when I welcomed Patricia back into our home to talk through, and plan, the approach to my adopted sister. I put the kettle on to make us some tea whilst she settled herself on the sofa, placed a briefcase on the seat beside her and opened the lid to reveal an impressive and orderly array of paperwork. As I sat down next to her she pulled out a loose-leaf file with my name printed on the front and opened it to reveal two sheets of paper. Withdrawing the top sheet she waved it triumphantly in front of me. I placed our hot drinks on the coffee table before taking it from her. It was a neat, handwritten letter on official headed notepaper, photocopied from the original with all identifying features of the recipient Tipp-exed out. Illegible, black smudges poked tantalisingly through the white Tipp-ex. Trembling slightly, I began to read what she had so carefully prepared for me.

Dear ....

I hope you may be able to help with an enquiry I have received. I do not know if you are aware that adoption law changed in December 2005 and birth relatives can now ask for an approach to be made to their relatives who were adopted. AAA NORCAP is a registered intermediary agency undertaking this work.

Jacqueline would welcome news of her sister who was born in 1942. The General register office has informed AAA NORCAP that Jacqueline's sister became ....

I would be grateful if you would contact me at the above address or phone number as I would like to discuss this enquiry with you. Please feel free to leave a message and your phone number on my answer phone if I am not in and I will return your call as soon as possible. I am usually available after 5 PM.

We were able to locate you using information provided by the General Register Office and publicly available records. I can assure you that Jacqueline is not aware of your name and address and will only learn of this if you give consent.

I enclose an AAA NORCAP leaflet that explains our work for your information.

I look forward to hearing from you.

Yours sincerely,

Patricia

I read it through twice to make sure I hadn't missed anything and to buy myself time before replying to Patricia. I was lost for words. Patricia was lovely and helpful and I knew I needed to muster up some thanks for her efforts, but I felt as though I was being denied access to a secret club of which I was a founder member. This was my special invitation to my sister yet it contained nothing of me. Must the tone be quite so sterile, the facts so starkly stated? My mentor was a pragmatist, yet gentle and kind. She understood the sensitivities on both sides of this wartime divide. Patiently she talked me through the reasoning behind the protocol and, though it would always seem harsh and alien to me, I did come to partially understand it. I had no choice.

I trusted Patricia but I was concerned for my sister. She would receive no prior warning and she would have no mentor to guide her through this initial approach. Her phone would not ring, her doorbell would not sound. The only intruder into her life would be my letter, a simple cold caller dropping through her letterbox on a bleak winter's day. And I would be completely to blame for any distress or upset this might cause her. The burden of responsibility weighed heavily once again.

Each person's experience of adoption is unique and there was no way of knowing what kind of relationship my sister had with her adoptive family or whether she would be receptive to contact from her birth family. Time alone would tell and Patricia could make no promises. But she was quick to reassure me, again, that the action I was taking was perfectly reasonable. She was also able to explain what would happen next if my sister didn't respond.

After one month a second letter, identical to the first, would be sent as a reminder. If that also failed to elicit a response then one month later a final letter would be sent. Patricia withdrew the second sheet of paper from my file and handed it to me. There was some comfort in the wording of this third attempt; it was a little less formal and did at least mention my disappointment at not having heard anything from her whilst informing her of the glimmer of hope that I still harboured that she might respond. Still, it seemed to me far too late and flimsy a testimony to the human cost of the whole process to be worthwhile at this stage. The only gift I was permitted to give my sister was time, and the liberty to take as much of it as she needed to reach her decision.

I thought back to my first meeting with Michele. There had been no intermediary to guide us at the start and it had been far from easy. It was our families who had provided the encouragement and support that ensured the success of our early progress. Charley and Sharon had furnished me with all the details I needed to approach Michele and my confidence came from their belief that I was doing the right thing. This felt so very different. But there was nothing I could do to alter the process, so I accepted Patricia's offer to send the first letter. She was delighted and agreed to post it the following Monday morning.

As the working week began, my imagination tracked the letter's journey down a thousand different paths; carried away on the wind, overlooked in the bottom of the post bag, chucked away with the rubbish … nothing was off-limits. Except perhaps a warm reception from its intended recipient, which I simply dared not believe possible.

So there I stood at the entrance to the tunnel with not a glimmer of light to guide me. Should I stride boldly forwards and lick my wounds if it all ended in tears? Or should I feel my way cautiously, shielding my hopes and protecting my dreams? It was the only control I had left. Either way, my sister held me at her mercy. She could take me by the hand and have us continue the journey together or she could send me spinning back into the darkness, with no hope for the future and no place of comfort to return to. The fairground would give me three chances at the game of patience. I was determined to get good at it.

The new school term had begun at a gallop. First up were A-level resit exams, closely followed by GCSE resits and beyond those lay a bewildering array of mock exams that would keep the school community busy until well into the spring. Just the thought of all that hard work ahead was exhausting on a cold, dark January evening. So I ran a bath to relax and prepare for our Tuesday ballroom dancing lesson which was guaranteed to lift my spirits. As the bath was filling my mind wandered back and forth to the letter. Where was it now? If Patricia had posted it in time it should have arrived today. Surely not this letter though? The whole process had taken so long, I couldn't imagine it speeding up any time soon.

Straining to hear above the noise of running water, I could hear the muted sound of the phone ringing downstairs. No need to rush to answer it, our landline seldom rang for me and I absentmindedly tried to recall which of Charlie's friends hadn't yet phoned him that evening.

Then, suddenly, Pete was shouting and my life was lurching forward. I raced down the stairs as he rushed to meet me halfway, almost dropping the receiver in his haste to pass it on. It was the final leg of the relay, I knew it now, as I took up the baton and raced towards the finishing line. I retreated with the phone to my own personal space as I tried to quell the panic and the threatening flood of tears. Whatever lay before me the wait was now over. My only line of defence was to hope for the best, prepare for the worst, and answer Patricia's call as calmly as I could.

CHAPTER 8

First Letters

"I HAVE SUCH GOOD news! She's phoned already! She phoned straight away!" Patricia sounded giddy with excitement. "We were on the phone for ages, she had lots of questions about everything and she is so easy to talk to. She sounds absolutely lovely," she paused, and when I replied I tried not to sound envious, I had to accept that the pace, for me, would be much slower.

"Wow, that's amazing! What can you tell me about her?"

"Her name is Pauline and she lives in the south of England. I can't tell you exactly where yet but, put it this way, it's a pretty easy place to get to. And you'll be pleased to know that she always knew she was adopted."

"Oh that's such a relief," I agreed.

"And she's happily married. She and her husband decided together that she should phone me. I have a really good feeling about this …" she was still joyous, but unable to tell me any more.

"And she didn't mind us contacting her?"

"Not at all, she seemed really pleased. I have told her that you won't be told her contact details until she is ready for you to have them, but that you will write to her as soon as you are able. It would be nice if you could include some photos of you and your family with that first letter. If that's possible?"

"Yes of course! I'll write to her immediately!" I said impulsively and with no thought as to how difficult that might prove, "and I'll get Pete to bring you the letter tomorrow if that's okay?"

"If he brings it in the morning I can catch the post at lunchtime. I'm so pleased for you. This really is an amazingly quick response."

"Thank you for all your kindness Patricia. I've been so lucky to have your help and guidance."

"It's what I'm here for. Now you'd better go. You have a letter to write!"

———

Sat at the kitchen table, with pen, paper and a mug of steaming coffee, my early morning routine lay broken all around me. I gazed out of the window and across the field to the coast road where a stream of cars carried early morning commuters towards their jobs in St Peter Port. On the table in front of me was a letter, faded with time, and written in pencil by a familiar hand. I had found it in an old white vanity case of my mother's that she kept under her side of the bed. Written on the day before Guernsey was liberated from the Nazis, it was Dad's first letter to Mum after the war. A genuine treasure.

The words seemed to flow effortlessly across the fragile, yellowed paper. Typical of my father who always took life, and all that it threw at him, in his stride. The war years had brought him few Red Cross letters from his wife but he had never once doubted that all would be well in the end. Now I had a first letter to write and I had no idea where to start.

I had been too tired from the emotion and relief of the phone call to compose anything the previous evening. Even now, refreshed by sleep, it remained a daunting task. But my sister had not kept me waiting and it was only fair to reciprocate. So I looked again at the sixty-five-year-old letter. Dad had known the person to whom he was writing, but he could have had no idea how their five years apart might have changed her. I would draw on his strength of character, remember his steadying hand on my life and allow his patience to empower me. And so, with Dad's spirit to guide me, I began to choose my first tentative words to reach out to my adopted sister.

Dear Pauline,

It is 6.15am on Wednesday 19th of January 2011 and I'm sitting with a cup of coffee and my dog at my feet wondering how to even begin my first letter to you? A letter to someone I've never met and yet is so important to me.

Well … here goes! First of all, thank you for responding so quickly to the letter from Patricia. When I embarked on trying to find you just over a year ago there were no guarantees and I've had to be very patient so thank you, thank you, thank you for being so quick, and it seems positive, in your response.

Ours is a long and complex story which I will happily share with you (as much as I know) if/when you are ready, but for now I will just say that up until 18 months ago I believed, and had no reason to believe otherwise, that I was an only child. Now, suddenly, at the age of 54, I have two sisters! It's wonderful! I know that Patricia has mentioned our other sister to you, her name is Michele, she lives in London and has three daughters. Her story is also a complex one and I've not been able to fully understand it yet, maybe I never will. The important thing for me is to move forward with what we have. One thing is for sure we are both thrilled to have found each other!

I have another 30 mins or so before I have to get ready for school! As you know, I'm a teacher – I teach at the local grammar school – mainly A-level mathematics. I'm going to find it very difficult to concentrate on my students today as my mind is elsewhere with you.

My first challenge, however, will be to get our 15-year-old son, Charlie, out of bed! He also attends the Grammar School which has not been without its problems for me! A budding rockstar, he doesn't quite have the academic application that the school expects. He is in Year 11 and has just had his mock exam results which actually don't seem as bad as we were perhaps expecting, so the hope is that this will spur him on to make an effort for the real things in the summer. He is a great lad... funny, thoughtful (in a teenage way) and surprisingly wise (at times).

My husband, Pete, is still in bed sleeping peacefully after the emotional evening we had yesterday. He is as pleased as I am to have made this initial contact with you. He keeps urging me to write a book ... maybe one day! Pete is retired so he can afford to stay in bed but I am soon going to have to reluctantly sign off.

Let me just tell you, though, of my daughter Anneka. She is 24 and a physiotherapist (very handy as I am riddled with aches and pains). She lives with her partner, Pete (yes very confusing) about half a mile up the road. We are very close and we see her a lot. She plays rugby (yes rugby!) and has always loved outdoor pursuits – particularly the dangerous, extreme kinds!

I paused in my writing, Mali was stirring at my feet, we were usually on the beach together at this time of the morning and she was getting restless. But today was a different kind of a day and she would have to wait until later. Instead, I made another cup of coffee and sat back down with a piece of toast to read through what I had written. Time was pressing and I needed to say goodbye to my sister.

Well, Pauline, it is now 7:15am and I am slightly more awake than when I started writing this. I've just read it back and am wondering if it will make any sense to you? Is this what you want to hear? Is the tone right? (Is the spelling right?!) I never handwrite anything any more! The truth is, of course, I don't know what you want to hear and

I don't know how to pitch it, but one day I believe that I will write this incredible story down and I hope very much that you will be a part of it – whatever part you want.

It is now 7:30am and I must dash! So I send to you, wherever you are, whatever part of the country you are waking up to this morning, my warmest wishes, all my love and a very big hug.

Jag x

CHAPTER 9

A Second Chance

We are standing in my parents' hallway, five of us now, on the way home from the hospital. Mum is wearing a bright blue polo neck jumper, it is the exact colour of her eyes which are shining with pride. Dad has his arm around her waist and is hugging her tightly towards him. We have popped in with our newborn, her very first excursion into the outside world.

The baby starts crying, the raw sound of the start of life. My mother is struggling now, to keep her emotions in check and to hold back the tears. I have never seen her like this, she despises outward shows of emotion. Has she waited too long for this moment? Though not once did she mention it?

I am mindful of her firstborn, my brother Michael, and wonder how her life might have been different had he lived. How my life might have been different too. The thought is quickly gone, she would not want it to hold me hostage. And with that, she lets me go, just as she has always done, back to my safely predictable world. And in return I let her go … back to face the demons that long ago locked up her secrets and threw away the key.

I am proud of my children and the extraordinary people they have become, they give my life its purpose and I know that the world will be in safe hands if only it will listen to them. Time played its tricks on me as I brought them up. It disguised its speed of passing as I lost myself to their purpose, encouraging me forwards, never allowing me to rest. Yet, however much I gave them, they gave me back more in return. I have boxes full of family photos that tell of our life together, happy times mostly, but sad and difficult times too. They remind me of the fun we had throughout the changing seasons, and how we gradually changed, too, throughout our lives. My children are adults now, and our recent photos are stored digitally, or uploaded onto social media. Sometimes, when browsing through the multitude of family groupings, I see what others have seen before me. The same tilt of the face, the same radiance in the smiles, the same squeeze of the eyes. A feast of nature and nurture, and more than a little of me, in the lives I have helped to create.

But I am not the source. For that, I must look back through the generations to the people that helped make me the person that I am. People that I am only just beginning to understand. I wonder how my mother felt on each of my sisters' birthdays? How she must have privately mourned the anniversaries of their parting? Had I known about them before her passing I could not have handled her pain. But she knew me too well and did not ask this of me. Instead, she took to her grave the skeletons of her past, and with that single tear, she left me, with my faith in the woman that she was, still intact.

Now life was bringing us a second chance. I hoped to build a bridge for us, strong enough to take the weight of Mum's memory and long enough to reach to the very heart of my adopted sister. It seemed the most, yet was the very least that I could do.

Pete delivered my letter to Patricia the next morning as promised and once again I found myself waiting. A couple of days later, as I entered the maths office at the end of break, the phone was ringing for me.

"She's replied!" said the familiar voice triumphantly. "There's a letter here for you! And she sent me one too, thanking me for all I had done. What a lovely person your sister is."

"That's wonderful. Can … " I paused to steady my voice, I had a lesson about to start. "Can I come and collect it at lunchtime? Around 1.15?"

"Of course. See you then."

The rest of the morning dragged its heels, refusing to be hurried by my impatience, and when the lunchtime bell finally rang I headed straight out of my classroom door ahead of all my students. By the time I reached Patricia's house, I was so full of nervous excitement I could barely function.

Patricia was full of warmth and kindness as she opened the door and welcomed me in. She sat me down at the dining-room table before sitting herself directly opposite, smiling kindly, checking I was okay before handing me the letter. Her calm exterior was impressive, but I could tell she was equally buoyant.

"I have a really good feeling about this. Do take your time to have a read and then maybe I could read it too? Pauline did request that you allow me to read it but, of course, you should read it first."

As I opened the envelope and removed its bulky treasures I felt hope, not just for myself and what the future might bring me, but for my mother too. Hope that, through me, she might finally be able to reach out to her long-lost daughter.

I was sitting across the dining table from Patricia who was feigning distraction but whom I knew was watching me intently. I skimmed through the letter which seemed warm and friendly, but I couldn't really take it in. Not here, not like this. But Patricia had invested in this journey, too, and was bound by protocol to support both Pauline and me on this final push towards reunion. I needed to stick to the rules.

"There you go." I managed a watery smile as I slid the letter across the table to her.

As she lost herself to Pauline's words, I was left to my own thoughts and the three photographs that had been carefully wrapped up inside the letter. The reality of her here in the palm of my hand seemed strange and surreal. The first photo had been taken on Christmas Day. Pauline was sitting on a sofa beaming up at the camera with a large pile of presents on her lap, all beautifully wrapped in gold paper and decorated with red ribbon. There was a serenity about her, a contentment with a life well-lived. The next one was of her daughter, Emma, crouching between two young boys in the garden; holding them close, all three looking and smiling directly at the camera. The third photo was of Pauline again, this time with her husband Ken, standing outside a hotel. They were dressed smartly, as if they were just about to go in for their evening meal, looking relaxed and happy.

Patricia handed me back the letter with a smile of genuine delight.

"Pauline seems such a lovely person. I really do think this is going to turn out well." She kept saying it. It must be true. I packed the letter and the photos back in their envelope and she showed me to the door. Her empathy and common sense had underpinned my quest; without her it would most likely have buckled and fallen. She would not be setting me adrift just yet and would continue to be our intermediary for a little while longer.

"Thank you, Patricia. I really do appreciate your support and your kindness. I'll be back with my reply as soon as possible."

She waited in the doorway until I was in the car with the engine running before giving me one final enthusiastic wave. It meant a lot to her that things were turning out well. Together we were victorious.

It was some time later, as I sat in a quiet spot just around the corner from Patricia's house, that I was able to answer the question that had been burning in my mind. Pauline reminded me of someone but I couldn't quite place who? I had expected Michele, but it was definitely not her. And it wasn't my mother either. My heart saw it first and danced with excitement. The tilt of her head, the radiance of her smile and the squeeze of her eyes ...

... suddenly I realised that, for the first time in my life, I was looking at a picture of a woman who looked very much like me!

CHAPTER 10

First Visit

IN ONE WAY OR another Pauline had dominated my thinking for most of the previous year. The emotional challenge that the search for her had entailed was far greater than I could ever have imagined. Thankfully I had struck lucky and she had been willing to make contact. But the rules were strict and I needed to stem my natural impatience in order to adhere to them. The letters would pass back and forth through Patricia until Pauline decided she was ready and willing to move to direct contact with me. The timescale was entirely in her hands. All I could do was comply.

In the meantime, I had my new relationship with Michele to nurture and develop and I needed to be equally patient with her. After our initial meeting, it seemed to be going from strength to strength. We spoke regularly on the phone and I visited her whenever I was staying in London, or flying off on holiday via one of the London airports. She was certainly pleased to see me, but our rendezvous were always held on neutral territory. There was never an invitation to her home or into her past and I, out of love and respect for her, didn't push for one. I had decided from the start that I would never ask for more than she was comfortably willing to give.

During the previous summer, I had persuaded her to visit us in Guernsey. She always referred to it so fondly as "home" that I was surprised, and somewhat saddened, to sense her considerable discomfort when she and her partner, Martin, first arrived to stay with us. Despite our best attempts to welcome them both, she seemed uneasy, unwilling, or perhaps just unable, to accept our hospitality. She declined our offer of food on the first evening preferring instead to take to her bed. Then, early the following morning, I woke to find her and Martin walking out of the house on a determined mission to find breakfast in one of the cafes or restaurants nearby. No amount of pleading could persuade her to stay, not even for a cup of tea. This left me feeling perplexed and uncomfortable. Life had been kind to me but I could sympathise with how tough it had been on her. I desperately wanted to try to make amends but it seemed that she was not going to make it easy for me.

Eventually, I accepted that it was me, and not her, that needed to change. I had to step back, bury my own agenda and take my cues from her. And then, slowly but surely, she began to relax in our home, and in my company, and we started to do things together, just as I had hoped.

I became the cautious tour guide, gauging my client's mood and tailoring her itinerary to suit. One day I took her into town for a stroll through our old neighbourhood, which she remembered well. Bosq Lane had changed almost beyond recognition in the five decades since we had both called it home, but the tiny terrace of three houses at the very top of the hill, on the right-hand side, had remained largely untouched. As we paused outside Romo, I lost her momentarily to the privacy of her past. She did not speak again until we found ourselves at the bottom of the hill where, still lost in her own thoughts, she pointed to the left and mumbled something about brother Peter. Try as I might I could not persuade her to part with any more information and, though I have since regretted not pushing harder for answers at the time, the reality was that she would almost certainly have refused to give them. Her past was a private space where intruders were not welcome. All I could expect from my sister was to walk beside her in the present towards whatever the future held for us.

Right from the start, Michele took a shine to Charlie. An obsession with music rather than school work had done little to endear him to his teachers, and his tendency to "clown around" meant that the school establishment had him earmarked as a trouble-maker. He saw the way he was being forced to learn as boring and mundane, whilst the school viewed him as underachieving and disruptive. But he was no rebel, it was simply that his interests and his talents lay outside of the academic. Michele came with me to Charlie's first-ever gig. It would turn out to be the first of many and, like me, she was very impressed by his performance. Charlie was unconventional and I think she saw a little of herself in him and loved him for it.

Whenever we touched on the past Michele spoke so fondly of her "daddy" that I could never find it in my heart to tell her that he could not be her biological father. She seldom mentioned Mum, though, and when I took her to pay her respects at my parent's grave she knelt to kiss the headstone, but only beside Dad's name. There seemed no way of persuading her to think more kindly of our mother. Just occasionally she would speak almost affectionately about her, but those moments were fleeting, and in general, she made it clear that she considered her a cold, merciless woman. Whilst perfectly understandable, this was difficult for me, and I think she understood that because, even though she held Mum accountable for the depth of her hurt, she never actively encouraged me to be disloyal to her.

Life had been hard on Michele and she, in return, was a little hard on life. We shared a mother and a brief collective past, but in every other respect, our lives were completely different. Resentment, injustice, privilege and favour swirled around us, searching for weakness and awaiting their opportunity to pounce; but they misjudged us. She had survived the inequity of her past by burying its reality and reimagining it in a more acceptable form. Whilst I, though desperate to uncover the secrets that lay buried within her story, considered the way forward far more important than the way back. For her part, she would not hold me to account, but she would never forgive our mother. I sensed that my nieces, too, were struggling to understand how any mother could abandon a daughter in the way they perceived our mother had abandoned Michele. They never actually said so for fear of hurting my feelings. Instead, they simply asked me:

'Why was she not given the same chance as Pauline?'

And it was a question that was impossible to answer to their satisfaction because their empathy was partisan whilst mine had been torn in two. I felt guilt at the privilege of my upbringing and shame that I could have so carelessly taken it for granted. I wished that I could have shared it with Michele. But I also felt pity for our mother, who had fallen victim to the cruel hypocrisies of her time. I could understand why, having lost two babies to natural causes and having given a third up for adoption, she might choose to leave her options open for her fourth.

It is early spring 1962. The weather is windy and cold and the pink and white blossom falls like snow from the cherry trees. I am shivering despite my red, winter coat. It is thick, with a furry collar and is well-worn as it is my only one. We are walking through the gardens in Bournemouth, three of us together, a chain of hands in hands. Every now and again I drop down, heavy on their arms, and they swing me high into the air. I am six and this is my first holiday.

We are staying in a house with two old ladies. Two very old ladies. They are kind to me and we play board games when Daddy needs to take Mummy for a drive. I don't think they have any children of their own. They give us cereal and toast in the mornings but in the evenings their kitchen is dark and empty and we go to a restaurant for our dinner. Mummy says it's okay to have beans on toast every night because we are on holiday.

They are talking about tomorrow, arranging what to do. They are going to meet someone and Daddy says they should take me with them. But Mummy is not so sure. I hope that I won't have to go because the old ladies have promised to play Monopoly with me ... but only if we have enough time.

Halfway through her visit Michele asked if she might have her birth certificate. Charley and Sharon had told her that I had sent for it. Of course I said yes, but it presented me with a dilemma. The certificate made no mention of my father whom she believed to be her father, too, and whom she clearly adored. Worse still it made no mention of any father. Fortunately, she soon forgot that she had asked for it and we were able to enjoy the rest of our time together without having to deal with the sadness that the truth might bring her. On her final day, I placed the birth certificate in an envelope, along with an explanatory letter and a painting of my father's, and slipped it into her suitcase just as I was about to take her to the airport. I hoped that she would read the letter quietly and privately, and that perhaps, as she reflected upon its contents, she might finally be able to make peace with the truth.

We hugged warmly at the airport, after a dodgy start it had turned into a really successful visit. As I waved her goodbye I told her about the certificate and she thanked me before disappearing through airport security. And then came the long wait to hear from her, and the worry as to how she might feel after reading my letter. Had I got the tone right? I resisted the urge to phone her straightaway and instead waited for her to approach me. And, though she never spoke to me directly about the contents of that letter, she did thank me for it and her gratitude was genuine because she was not the kind of person who would spare someone's feelings by hiding any displeasure.

From time to time she would refer to what I had written, saying just enough to reassure me that she had read the letter through carefully and that she had understood its contents. And I knew that she kept it safely, in the silver box I had given her one birthday. It was a relief to know that it had not divided us as I had feared but instead had edged us a little closer together, just as I had hoped.

CHAPTER 11

Pauline

BEFORE LONG, AND AT her suggestion, Pauline and I moved to communicating directly via email. It felt ungrateful and a bit sad to bypass Patricia at first but, just as wise parents know that they cannot hold on to their children forever, so Patricia knew that our relationship needed to develop and move on without her. She had successfully brought us together and now was the time for her to let us go.

Electronic communication made our lives much easier and brought us into each other's homes on a daily basis. One of Pauline's first requests was for me to send her a photo of Mum which I was delighted to do. I considered this a very good sign. It was early days, but she didn't seem to harbour any animosity towards Mum. Instead, she showed a genuine, if somewhat casual, interest in her that I found easy to satisfy.

We were both eager to learn details about the other's family and friends and gradually we revealed our lives to each other through the exchange of photographs, news and pleasantries. She was generous with her time and warm in her writings, but she held back on giving me any further contact details, and made it gently but firmly clear that the time and distance that email exchanges gave us suited her needs perfectly.

After a while, this started to worry me. Impatience started to creep into our home and Pete once again found it increasingly difficult to understand why I refused to simply ask for her telephone number. For a long time, I remained determined that it must be she who moved to the next stage first. But eventually, impatience got the better of me, too, and I judged enough time should have passed for me to try to ease things on a little. I sent her my contact details, in their many and varied forms, and invited her to phone me, if and when she felt ready, along with a humble apology if this seemed in any way too "pushy". As soon as I pressed "send" I questioned the sense of my action, but I had left myself no choice but to sit back and wait. Almost immediately the email conversation between us dried up and, though the phone in our house continued to ring constantly, for a long time it was never for me.

At first, I was disorientated by the call. Pete was off-island and Charlie and I had arrived home just as the sun was setting on a particularly beautiful spring day right at the end of the Easter Term. We were hungry and cold, and each carrying bags spilling school books and shopping, as we pushed our way through the unlocked back door and into the kitchen. The phone had been ringing for some time when I tripped over the dog in my rush to grab it, expecting it to be Pete. The rise and fall in the unfamiliar melody of her west country lilt caught me off balance and, though I knew immediately it was her, it still had the power to take my breath away. She sounded very different to Michele, very different to me and I was so enchanted by her accent that I found it quite difficult to concentrate on what she was actually saying.

"I'm so sorry I haven't called sooner. You must have thought I was never going to ring. Is this a good time?"

"Hello! It's so good to hear from you. Of course it's a good time!"

"I can call back another time if it's better for you?" She still wasn't sure. But any time was good for me and it wasn't long before we settled into easy dialogue, which was certainly a relief but perhaps should not have surprised either of us. We had lost too many years already for us to tolerate any awkward silences.

I was on a real high when the call finally came to an end. We had chatted for a long time and had reluctantly left each other with the promise that we would talk again soon. No sooner had I put the phone down than I picked it up again. It was always hard to predict how Michele might feel about anything but she was as close as I was to this particular story and it was her that I wanted to share it with first. She sounded excited to hear that I had spoken to our sister and eager to learn what had been said, and I considered that a good start. I hoped that, in time, the two of them might speak directly. For now, though, I knew that it must fall to me to act as an intermediary.

Sleep did not come easily that night. How could anyone relax after speaking to their sister for the first time? How was I supposed to feel? Over the past few weeks she had become increasingly real, to the point that I could almost reach out and touch her, but we were not quite there yet. The letters had been great, the emails too and the phone call was just wonderful, but still I wanted more. How was she feeling? She had sounded so gentle and calm on the phone, balanced and in complete control. Whereas I had been left struggling to steady myself. The next day I dropped her a quick email before going to school, thanking her for the call and telling her how much it had meant to me. And I was delighted to receive a response later that same day, though it wasn't from her:

Hello Jag

I'm afraid you will have to put up with a quick reply from Pauline's P.A. tonight. Actually, we only picked up your mail a short while ago, and she just had time to read it before leaving for her badminton session, so she's asked me to send a quick reply. Unfortunately, my keyboard skills are fairly basic so it will take me ages!

She was really on a high last night, both before (quite nervous) and after (excited) chatting to you. Making contact by phone was the next obvious step for you both, and I think that she is pleased that the ice has now been broken in this way. Before she called, she said that perhaps I might like to say "hello" to you, but that was soon forgotten once the two of you started chatting. No doubt, my turn will come at some point in the future.

Well I'm going to close now. I need to prepare fresh strawberries and yoghurt before I pick up Pauline. We always have our main course at about 5.30 and then our dessert later in the evening while we are watching telly.

Don't work too hard. Just reading about your typical busy day makes me feel tired!

Take care
Ken xx

It was lovely to receive this warm, friendly email from my new brother-in-law and it was reassuring to hear that my sister seemed as emotionally invested in the whole process as I was.

As the weeks passed we spoke regularly on the phone which proved a wonderful way of getting to know each other better. Our inboxes had been full to bursting with details of the paths down which our lost years had taken us, but they were no substitute for a nice long chat. All that groundwork had provided us with an excellent understanding of each other's lives, however, and it meant that we could live together in the present without having to constantly revisit and explain the past. Sometimes we allowed our husbands in on our conversations but mostly we just chatted to each other about our family, our friends and our busy lives. She was refreshingly easy to talk to and the bond between us grew stronger with each call.

Although she didn't look like Mum in the way Michele did, or sound like her, there was something about Pauline that reminded me very much of our mother. For a long time, I struggled to pinpoint exactly what it was. Perhaps it was her sense of humour? We both saw the funny side in ordinary everyday happenings and laughter was the medium that allowed us both to sparkle. Eventually, I understood that it was not in a single quality that she was like Mum, but in the whole package. She was attractive, kind and full of fun, and she cared selflessly for elderly relatives and friends when they were ill or had fallen on hard times. And, just like Mum, Pauline seemed to live her life entirely through routines whereas I tended to live mine around them. She also seemed able to hold back a small part of herself, to act as an anchor against the currents of life, whereas my openness meant that I would always be vulnerable to the flow of the river and therefore far more easily swept away.

Before I knew it the May half-term holiday was upon us. Pete and I had made no particular plans until Charlie received an unexpected invitation to go to London with a friend and we suddenly realised that we had a few days on our own. On the spur of the moment I wrote to her.

Hi Pauline,

A quick but not necessarily an easy question! How would you feel about us meeting?!

The reason I ask is that Charlie is going to London with a friend from Monday till Wednesday which leaves Pete and I free to go away without fear of what we leave behind! I've just checked the ferries and it looks like we could come over with the car arriving in Weymouth early afternoon on Monday and leaving Weymouth at mid-day on Wednesday. We have friends who live in Wiltshire and also friends who live outside Bristol and we would probably stay with them. However, the main reason for our visit would be to meet you - if you feel you are ready to meet.

This is very last minute and may not even be a possibility for all sorts of reasons but I thought I'd sound you out. You mustn't be in the least bit worried about upsetting me if you don't feel it's the right time to meet because it wouldn't upset me – just be honest with how you feel about it and I will understand.

Will give you a ring over the weekend, just didn't want to put you on the spot about above question on the phone.

Lots of love to you both,
Jag xxxx

Her reply giving me the green light was not immediate and she was right when she said that I must have thought that she was not yet ready to meet up. Nevertheless, she gave me just about enough time to make a booking, pack a few clothes and organise a dog-sitter. So, for the second time in as many years, I started to prepare myself for a meeting with a new sibling.

I packed the car full of anticipation, hope and a few carefully chosen items of new clothing to ensure that I would look and feel my best. I had a reasonable idea as to what to expect in terms of the emotional journey I was about to make and it made sense to do whatever I could to make the physical journey as smooth as possible. Pete and I shut up the house and set off for the harbour in silence. The opportunity had arisen too late for us to make it into anything other than a fleeting visit, but it was a start.

Time kicked its heels as the ferry lumbered unenthusiastically across the English Channel towards Weymouth and it wasn't until late in the day that we found ourselves on the road and heading towards Bradford-on-Avon. We had chosen the location carefully for its respectful distance from my sister, its ease of proximity for us both and its reputation as a natural beauty spot which would lift our spirits should we find ourselves in need of that kind of boost. I had no wish to repeat the gloomy experience of the hotel in London where I had felt like a caged animal. Bradford-on-Avon also happened to be where Pauline's daughter Emma lived.

It was four months already since Pauline had received the initial letter from Patricia and my feelings were struggling to keep pace with my thoughts as we drove through the English countryside on our way to finally meet her. The past two years had been exhilarating and full of joy, but they had been challenging too. Though I welcomed the challenge, I had not yet learned how best to fully embrace it. Nor had I learned how to control the voice in my head that constantly questioned whether I was being disloyal to my mother. She had taken to her grave secrets of such unbearable magnitude that I feared

I might destroy her very essence if, by my digging, I should unleash even more animosity towards her. Mum had buried Pauline so deeply in the past that I wasn't even sure that Dad had known about her.

It was wonderful to be reunited with Michele after all these years and I loved her dearly but I naturally felt sad and uncomfortable at the way she despised our mother. What if Pauline, like Michele, felt hostility towards her birth mother? From what I knew of her so far I very much doubted she would, but still I spent most of the journey questioning my motives and wondering if I really was, after all, doing the right thing.

Night fell, unnoticed, as we approached our hotel, and the kitchens had long since closed so there was no chance of food. But the welcome was warm and extended to a glass of wine in the bar which worked quickly to smooth away the frayed edges of my nerves. Our room was calm and quiet and darkened by a row of trees outside the windows, that hung low over the river smothering out the streetlights. The journey had tired us and we were both grateful for the warmth and comfort of the bed. Within minutes Pete had fallen into a deep untroubled sleep, whilst I tucked myself under the duvet and prepared for the long wait until morning.

After a welcome breakfast, we meandered through the narrow streets of the charming old town and strolled along the banks of the swollen river before heading back towards our hotel. At Ken's suggestion, we were to meet by the bridge nearby. It was an easy location for us and there was plenty of parking nearby for them. We arrived a few minutes early and found ourselves a vacant seat beside the bridge from where we could watch and wait. An endless stream of cars passed by, their occupants vacant and disinterested, travelling mindlessly through their unexceptional days. But I was on fire and she was too so when our paths did finally cross we were easily recognisable. As I caught my first glimpse of her through the car window she raised her hand, as did I, and with that first wave, we welcomed in the start of our extraordinary day.

Their car disappeared up a nearby hill and within minutes they were walking down the road hand in hand, their welcome reaching towards ours with hugs and excited greetings that were warm and sincere. She was tall, though not as tall as me, and slim and she was dressed in one of my favourite colours, a pastel shade of purple that perfectly complemented her flawless complexion and offset her stunning silver hair.

For a moment we wondered what we should do. They had booked a table for lunch in a nearby country pub but it was still only mid morning. We decided to walk to our hotel for a coffee. With all that we had in common, we were assured of a conversation that would flow, though none of us had any idea in which direction it might take us. The waiter brought us our coffee and then left us to it, unaware of the enormity of the occasion, and that was precisely what we needed.

We exchanged a few pleasantries and our excitement at meeting each other at last, and then Pete and Ken settled into an easy conversation about fishing. With my sister by my side, I was ready to go a little deeper, if she was willing.

"It was such a relief to me that you knew that you were adopted," I ventured. "Imagine if you had received my letter and you hadn't known. I really worried about that!"

"Yes, I always knew ... but I can't actually remember anyone ever sitting down with me to tell me. When Ken and I got married, my sister gave me my adoption papers for safe keeping."

She paused but I said nothing. Hoping; willing her to say more.

"I read all the letters at that time but didn't think it would ever be possible to find out any more details about my birth mother. It never even crossed my mind that I could possibly have any brothers or sisters."

I had so many questions but I held them all in, determined not to interrupt her and break her train of thought.

"I filed all of the papers away and, almost 50 years later, we read them when I received your first letter. I hadn't even shown them to Emma before that. It was quite sad, really, because I didn't even have a name at that time. I was referred to as 'baby Le Bargy.' Emma said it sounded as though I was a parcel to be collected."

I thought of Mum, looking after Pauline whilst the process of her adoption swung irrevocably into motion. A process that she wouldn't have wanted but that she must have agreed to.

"In one letter it actually said that there was a baby girl for them to collect and would they please bring a warm shawl with them. We tried picturing them catching the train carrying a shopping bag containing this "warm shawl", and then returning home on the train with me all snugly wrapped up! I was just two months old when they brought me home."

It was my turn to speak but it took me a long time to find the courage to ask her.

"Do you know anything about your father?"

"No! Only that he was twenty years old when I was born."

Whether her adoption papers were scant on detail or whether she simply chose not to share the finer details with me I couldn't be sure. For all her warmth and kindness I sensed that Pauline, like Michele, was a very private person, so I gratefully accepted what she offered and focused, instead, on nurturing our relationship.

It was Pauline who practised the word "sister" first, as she and I negotiated the narrow corridors of the hotel in search of the bathroom. I was thrilled to hear it, but it was a term that held such magnitude for me that I shied away from using it quite so casually. She had grown up with an adoptive sister, sixteen years her senior, so the concept was not as new to her as it was to me. I found myself needing a little more confidence before I could articulate such hope.

Before we knew it we were walking to the car for Ken to drive us to the country pub. The venue they had chosen was cosy and intimate and we took time over lunch to relax and enjoy each other's company. After lunch, Pauline asked if we would like to go to her daughter, Emma's house for tea. She and her husband were teachers and were also on their half-term break, so this was a welcome but unexpected bonus.

The afternoon passed in a haze of love and laughter, captured on camera and recorded with fondness in a special place in all our hearts. We spent most of it in their garden, under a paraphernalia of umbrellas and sunshades erected in haste to protect us from some English summer rain. We got on so well that it was hard to imagine that we had all been strangers until recently.

All too soon it was time for us to leave but first, we were invited to take a quick look at some photos on the family computer. We relocated to the family room which, Pauline observed with pleasure, or perhaps relief, had been specially tidied for our visit. It had all the makings of a comfortable, if chaotic space, and one in which I felt very much at home. As we huddled around the computer, waiting for the photos to load, I took a long look around the room searching out the story that the four walls contained. The warmth of family love was palpable and there was plenty of evidence of the hobbies that were encouraged and the talents supported. In one corner was a drum kit and various musical instruments lay scattered around the room. Charlie's music provided the backdrop to our lives in Guernsey so I felt I was amongst kindred spirits here. Photos, books and souvenirs surrounded me, this was definitely my kind of room.

And then, suddenly, my eyes were stilled as I saw it, and the nagging voice in my head was finally brought under control as I teetered on the verge between laughing and weeping. She had been here with us all along and I wondered how I could ever have doubted it. Standing, in pride of place, in the centre of Emma's mantelpiece, was a beautifully framed photograph of Mum.

CHAPTER 12

Nana

THE JOURNEY BACK TO Guernsey the next day was long and uneventful and gave me plenty of opportunity for reflection. Pete was driving and was in a buoyant mood.

"I can't believe how alike the two of you are. I mean we always knew you looked alike from all the photos, but you are even more alike in real life. You even have the same mannerisms!"

"Do you think so? I certainly felt a real connection with her. In what ways did you think we were the same?"

The countryside rolled past as he reeled off his list of observations. He had been my rock throughout all of this and, though he sometimes found my responses difficult to gauge, he could not be faulted for his unconditional support for me, my sisters and our mother.

I wondered how Pauline was feeling today? My thoughts started to flicker, back and forth between my two new families, and then to my familiar one back home. Finally, they settled on Mum, out of reach now but very much in the midst of us all. So there we stood, Michele, Pauline and I, victims of our personal diaspora, long since orphaned and left to make sense of it all.

———

There is always a buzz of excitement on board the ferry as it approaches the islands of the Bailiwick. No sooner had the strong currents swept us past Alderney than the white-shelled sandy beaches of Herm began to appear on the horizon, flanked by the silhouettes of Sark and Jethou. Soon the visual feast reached its finale as the ferry slowed almost to a standstill and we entered the harbour. There could be no greater welcome home for me today, or for my mother all those decades before, than the site of the picturesque town of St Peter Port lying nestled on the hillside in front of us.

Charlie was already back from his London trip and Anneka was also at home to greet us. We waited impatiently for Pete to upload our camera full of photos onto the computer. They didn't disappoint. The fun, the love and the laughter had survived the journey. After the excitement of the previous few days, I found myself in urgent need of sleep, but there were two people that I needed to make contact with before I could have any hope of rest. I picked up the phone to call Michele and, as soon as I had replaced the receiver, I penned a quick email to Pauline.

1st June 2011 22:22

Hi Pauline,

I have just spoken to Michele to tell her about our meeting. I wanted to phone her straight away as I didn't want her to feel left out – I know she'd like us all to meet one day.

Well, I am still on a high! It was wonderful to meet you and Ken at last and meeting Emma, Andy and the boys was a real bonus. What a lovely family you all are and I was so touched by the picture of Mum on her mantle-piece – I can't tell you how much that meant to me.
I know what you mean about worrying what we might say to each other and would we get on. I worried a little bit too, but my real concern has always been that my search for my sisters, which is wonderful for me, might be being selfishly disloyal to mum. The pain

of her loss overwhelms me at times and I guess I feel a bit guilty that I can meet you and build a relationship with you and your family which she was never able to do. She is central to our relationship and yet somehow excluded from it. So to see her picture in Emma's house, and to know that Em cares enough to put that picture there, was hugely reassuring. I feel very good about everything and I hope that you do too.

Could you please give me Emma's email address – I'd like to thank her.

Off to wipe my eyes and blow my nose!

Big hug
Jag
xxxx

It was the first time I had opened up to her in this way, but I judged it was time and the email that arrived the next day was as full of emotion and hope for our future as mine had been to her. She had her own feelings of guilt and so could empathise with mine. However, we both knew that life must go on and that, when it takes such an unexpected turn, the wisest response is to embrace all that the new direction has to offer.

Pauline told me that Mum's picture had been on Emma's mantelpiece from the day I first sent it to her. She had never had a grandmother so to have a share in Anneka and Charlie's was very special to her. Like Emma, to have a share in a new family was very special to me, and I counted myself fortunate to have found two new families and to have been welcomed into both. They had already enriched my life in more ways than I could ever have imagined, but I owed my mother loyalty, and I felt uncomfortable embracing a happiness that had been gained at her expense. The signs from Pauline and Emma on that score were good.

In the days that followed, I wrote to Emma, to thank her for the warmth of her welcome and her generosity of spirit. Emma's reply, when it came, further empowered me to reach beyond my fear of betrayal and embrace whatever happiness our future might bring.

Sunday, 5th June 2011

Hi Auntie Jag,

Mum read out your email - and I had tears in my eyes too! The picture of Nana has been there ever since you emailed them to Mum, and I printed them out for her. The thing about Nana is that she always makes me smile! And I can't look at the photo without a grin on my face. At the end of the day Auntie Jag, and I've said this to Mum - especially on Monday night when she was worried about meeting up with you - no one can take away what she has now. You have come into our lives now, and for whatever reason, the timing has been right. I don't think Mum would have been able to handle this before now - with Auntie Hazel being so ill. If things had been different, she wouldn't have met my Dad, I wouldn't be who I am, and my whole existence with Andy and the boys would never have happened. Society back in Nana's day was cruel - people would not have understood the situation and I am sure that it was the only thing Nana could do - it wouldn't have been the easiest decision to make and I am sure Mum (and indeed Michele) were always in her thoughts. I am a very strong believer in fate - and what will be, will be! We can't change history - it's probably best that we can't in some cases - but it is so wonderful that we have all now met up and are part of one another's lives. It seems so strange that last Christmas we knew nothing of one another and now look at us!

As for giving Mum the green light - she made up her own mind - all I said was, if it works out we have new blood in our lives, if it doesn't work out, we have nothing to lose! She knew I would support her whatever - I'm just so pleased that she went with her heart and replied to Patricia's letter. As long as she realised that no one could take away anything that she already had - the boys mean everything to her - maybe as an only child I have an extra special bond with Mum and Dad - maybe more so with Mum after her childhood. But whatever the reasons IT'S ALL WORKED OUT FOR THE BEST!!!!! I'm sure Anneka would agree with me as well!

The thing that I loved on Tuesday was that it was as if we did know one another - it felt the most natural thing in the world to be sat talking to you and Uncle Pete - Andy said the same. If we had met you on holiday we would have kept in touch, we are the same sort of people and that's why it worked. All I can say is thank you so much for finding Mum - it must have been such a difficult decision for you - shall I shan't I? Will she or won't she? It's a mad, mad world we live in - and luckily you took the plunge!!!!!

Take care, love to Uncle Peter, Anneka and Charlie

Lots of love
Em and the boys xxx

PART THREE

The house was completely silent, the entire family, including the dog, having been told to keep well out of the way. At precisely 10am I lifted the receiver to a complete stranger, a kindly-sounding old man with a picture of me in front of him; the sole reference for the call. I held my breath, to listen was paramount. One by one they came, the whispers of the past, Dad leading the way just as he always did. A weightless, silent audience of eager contributors most of whom I recognised; a few I couldn't place.

It was some time later, when the recording arrived in the post with the caption on the front, that I understood the significance of the date. At 10am on the 10th day of the 10th month of the 10th year of the new millennium our worlds did indeed pass close enough for questions to be answered. Not necessarily the questions on my agenda, but subtle questions of far greater significance answered to our mutual satisfaction.

We knew, we understood and we were sorry.

CHAPTER 1

Mother Hubbard Is Always With Us

MOST PEOPLE WHO EMBARK on a journey have a rough idea, at least, of where it might take them. Since the first email from Charley Miller, on Friends Reunited, I had embarked on several journeys simultaneously without the slightest idea where any of them might lead. They buoyed me up and tossed me around on waves of relentless uncertainty to which I surrendered completely in the vain hope of securing closure and peace.

Both my sisters seemed equally invested in the journey that lay ahead, though they tended to pull the narrative in slightly different directions which resulted, perhaps inevitably, in me having two paths to follow rather than one. Each seemed content to entrust to me our progress and I took care to modify its pace to reflect the needs of the slowest participant. Welcoming them into my life, even at this relatively late stage, had been easy. But these were people who should have been there from the start, so the pull backwards, in search of what had gone wrong, felt especially strong. It was challenging for all of us, albeit in different ways, and many times I found myself negotiating rough tracks, or entering blind alleys, that my sisters were reluctant to commit to. So I was the constant, and often the lonely, passenger.

I had always considered my memory to be sharp, but the discovery of my new families called it so ruthlessly to account that the whole fabric upon which it had been based seemed to crumble beneath the weight of such scrutiny. No amount of probing or persuasion could push my thoughts back further than they wanted to go, and I was constantly left wondering why I had so few tangible memories of Michele.

Nor could I remember many details about Dad's stories of the Occupation, though he never lost his enthusiasm for telling them. They would fascinate me now, but as a child I grew weary of hearing them, considering them little more than black and white images of a two-dimensional past. Likewise, Mum's experiences of evacuation; I never thought to question her reluctance to share them, to me that just seemed natural for a woman who tended to live her life in other people's shadows.

My parents were the living history books that I chose not to read. I considered myself the leading lady, not just in my own life, but in their lives too, and I never thought to remind myself that they had once held centre stage before me. To me, Mum and Dad were just creatures of routine, people who did their weekly shop on a Tuesday, went out for a bar meal with friends every Friday and cooked lunch for me and my family on a Sunday.

The discovery of my sisters changed everything. It swept me back to the start of our universe to search for the answers that lay buried in the fragments of those first few moments. In the fourteen years since Dad had passed, three out of the four removals boxes that Pete had packed away remained untouched in our attic. The time had come to free the spirits of the lives they contained.

By mutual agreement, we decided I should open the boxes in our garden room, a cheerfully chaotic space where a bit of dust would go unnoticed and where there was ample room for me to lay out the contents and take my time looking through them. By the time I had made us some tea Pete was already slicing through the brown tape on the first box with his pocket knife. Hot pink, bougainvillea flowers cascaded down the exposed granite wall behind him whilst overhead, the thick, leafy vine filtered out the ferocity of the sun and allowed a gentle, dappling of light to dance on the old sofa below; our garden room was my happy place.

The air was thick with excitement and anticipation as Pete peeled back the lid on the first box whilst I sat, perched on the end of my seat, waiting for my nerves to steady and my hands to stop shaking. But I didn't hold back for long. Before I knew it I was coughing and sneezing my way through the contents of the box as the dust of their lives caught in my throat.

My dad it seemed, had kept everything from electricity bills, to details of the vegetables he had planted in his allotment, to the receipt for Mum's wedding ring. He kept diaries of the weather, of how many units of electricity were generated at the power station each day and of the weekly petrol consumption of his cars. He must surely have kept some details regarding Michele?

I paused in my search. All around me the flamboyant colours of my present swirled above the flecked hues of their past; the heady perfume of now, the muted mustiness of then. The bundles of old-fashioned bills and receipts brought memories of the long-forgotten, and stoked the embers of a nostalgia that still lived deep within me. In an old, hard-backed notebook, I found my dad's transcript of a wartime play. The spine of the book had long since disintegrated leaving the covers held in place by the thinnest of threads, but the elegance of Dad's handwriting had survived the years. The steady, unwavering flow of the script reminded me of the influence he had had on my life. The rise and flow of each letter, gently and lovingly stroking the page just as he had stroked away every one of my childhood tears.

It wasn't until I reached the bottom of the box that I got my first real breakthrough. In a brown leather case I found dozens of Red Cross letters, sent between Mum and her loved ones in Guernsey during the war. There was a neglected, fragility about them that suggested they had fulfilled their purpose and been gently laid to rest. But my mission was new and burning; I swept them from their crypt, settled back onto the sofa and began my journey through them.

Enthusiasm quickly turned to disappointment, however, as I realised that these tiny bundles of narrative had survived to tell their tale for one simple reason, they gave nothing away. I was about to put them back into their case when I noticed three small postcards that I had overlooked earlier. Printed at the top of each card was the word "Internierungslager" (internment camp).

In September 1942, everyone in Guernsey aged 16-70, and born in England, was deported to Internierungslager in Europe, in retaliation for the British internment of Germans living in Persia. In the bottom left-hand corner was the name of the internee, (an old family friend of the Loveridge family), and the address of Biberach Internment Camp.

Turning the cards over I found each to be crammed full of tiny pencilled words, crawling along lightly ruled lines, and squeezed as tightly together as possible to maximise their disclosure. The script was faded and unfamiliar, but I could just about make out that each card carried a carefully transcribed message from my grandparents in Guernsey to their daughters in Bridgwater.

As I finished reading the third card my mood lifted. Like the Red Cross messages, the cards did not hold the answers to any of my questions. Of course they didn't! My expectations had been wholly unrealistic. But these messages, though flimsy in content, were the only communication between my mum in the

UK, and her family in Guernsey, for the entire duration of the war. They must hold a representative, if not intimate, timeline of those five years. I rearranged the whole lot into chronological order and, as I re-read them, I disciplined myself to look between the lines, to identify gaps and to focus on the unwritten rather than the written. In this way the story progressed, by following cautious reason and in the absence of hard proof.[6]

Guernsey 7.4.1941
Everyone cheerful. Don't worry. Kathleen Ann born August 16.
All love Mummie

Bristol 30.10.1941
Dearest Mum and Dad, Happy Christmas. You are always in our thoughts. We are well.
Best love Kath and Dink

Guernsey 30.10.1941
Dear Kath, Everyone here okay. How are you? Always thinking of you. Wish we were together darling. Mother Hubbard often with us.
Love Charles.

Bristol 30.10.1941
Dear Charles, hope you are well and happy. Please write. We are well. Always thinking of you.
All love Kath
Guernsey 26.11.1941
Had messages (2) from Dinkie. Glad you are well, everyone here same. Writing possible. Wish we were together. Keep your chin up Darling.

---

6   For details of the Red Cross Message Service, see Exhibit B.

Love Charles.

Taunton 27.11.1941

Dearest Charles, Hope you are well. My thoughts are always with you. Please write. Anxious for news.

Best love Kath

Bristol 4.12.1941

Dearest Mum and Dad, Have only had one message from you. Anxious for news. How are you? Don't worry all well.

Love Kath.

Guernsey 26.2.1942

Darling Kath, Still awaiting news from you. I am fit and well, longing to see you again. How about request Sandy's half hour.

Charles

Guernsey 14.3.1942

My Darling Received second message, three from Dinkie. We all write monthly, are you together? All well here, write Peggy.

Dearest love Mum, Dad, Maurice.

Guernsey 26.3.1942

Dear Kath Received your message October. I am OK. Still in same job. What are you doing? Always thinking of you.

Love Charles.

England 2.4.1942

Delighted to get message. Miss you too honey. Look after yourself I worry about you. Am quite well and still working.

All my love.

Guernsey 19.5.1942
Getting more news from you lately. Glad you OK. Am thinking of you always. So keep smiling blue eyes.
Love Charles.

Guernsey 21.5.1942
My dear little girls, Hope well, here well, miss you very much. Keep smiling. Are you working?
From your old Dad dearest love. Mummie, Maurice.

England 23.6.1942
My Dearest Charles, Don't worry about me. I'm fit and working. Do you receive my messages? Miss you terribly. Wish we were together.
Fondest love Kath

Guernsey16.6.1942
Dear Kath, Received 2 messages this week. April 2nd. Don't worry I'm OK. Irene has baby girl. Starting holidays today. Very quiet here.
Love Charles.

England 7.7.1942
My darling Charles, Don't worry. I'm quite fit and working. Look forward to your messages every month. Miss you terribly.

Guernsey 9.7.1942
Getting more news lately. Everyone here OK. Taking up stage work in spare time. First show October. Writing you monthly, keep smiling,
Love Charles.

England 7.8.1942
My dearest Charles, terribly worried about you. We are both quite fit and working. Keep smiling honey. Miss you terribly.
Love Kath.

England 7.8.1942
Darling Mum and Dad, Dinkie happily married. Nice reliable fellow. Sure you will approve. Known him two years. Gave consent for Daddy. Still together.
Kathy

England 7.8.1942
Dear Peg, Dinkie happily married. Lots of old friends turned up at church. We are still with Auntie Lil. How are babies and Charlie?
Love Kathy

Guernsey 16.9.1942
Just finished first show, great success. Looking forward to next one. No news lately from you. Hope you are OK. Keep smiling Darling.
Love Charles.

Guernsey 14.10.1942
No news from you lately. Everyone here OK. Life very boring. Miss you more than ever Darling. Best wishes for Christmas.
Fondest love Charles.

Guernsey 13.11.1942
Still no news from you lately. Hope you are OK. Appearing in musical show next week. Everyone here OK.
Love you as always Darling. Charles.

Guernsey 9.12.1942

Writing you monthly. Do you receive my messages? Hear from you rarely. Hope you are OK. Love you more than ever Darling. Christmas greetings. Charles.

Guernsey 14.12.1942

My darlings, Great surprise. Did not know Dinkie was courting. Satisfied if you approve. What is new name. Best luck. Fondest love, Mum, Dad, Maurice.

Guernsey 15.12.1942

Dear Kathie, Congratulations Dinkie and husband. Longing see you all. Tell Dinkie write, don't forget us. Babies, Charlie well. Writing monthly. Maureen born September.

Guernsey 15.12.1942

Thrilled with news, first for months. Don't worry about me am OK. Look after yourself Darling. Longing to see you. Congratulations to Dinkie.

Love Charles.

Guernsey 23.12.1942

Darling Kath, Glad to get news. Doing stage work in spare time. Pegging along with chin up.

Keep smiling Darling and lots of love Charles.

Guernsey 20.1.1943

Still sticking it. Hope you are doing the same. Hope you've still got my suit. Need it badly. Always thinking of you. Here's hoping.

Love Charles.

Guernsey 16.3.1943
My Darlings, Hope all well. Longing for news. All well here. Kept busy with babies. Write often. Praying for reunion.
Fondest love Mummy, Dad, Maurice.

Guernsey 14.4.1943
No news for some months. Hope you are OK. Everyone here OK. Plenty of sunbathing. Still at Romo, lucky so far. Keep smiling.
Love Charles.

England 20.4.1943
My Darling, Received your message today our anniversary. Hope it is good luck. Everything OK. Happy Birthday. Keep smiling honey.
Love you more than ever Kathy.

Guernsey 12.5.1943
Thinking of you always. Everyone here OK. Tucker leaving us after two years poor health. Longing for reunion. Here's hoping soon.
Love Charles.

13.5.1943
My own darlings, Hope all well. Heard Dinkie baby son through June Gray. If so congratulations. Big kiss baby.
Dearest love. Mum, Dad, Peggy, Maurice.

Biberach Internment Camp, Germany. 6.6.43
Dear Kath and Dinkie you will be surprised to hear from me, I had a letter from your mum with your address and she asks me if I would write you. She would like you to write to me so I can send her more details how you are. If you write a letter to your mum I will copy it and send on. Hope you are keeping well. We are fine. Your mum says they get very few messages from you, I expect they get lost. Have had 27 letters from June and photo since we've been here. If you have any photo for your mum I can let her have them. Peggy has three fine children. Mum sends you her love also Dad. Your mum says she can hardly believe Dinkie is married, you are still a baby to her but time passes and you all get so grown up.
Best Auntie Ethel.

Guernsey 11.6.1943
Have you still got my suit! Clothes here a problem, nothing new since you left. Family and self O.K. No news you 6 months.
Charles.

Guernsey 9.7.1943
No news since last August. Very anxious. All well here. Longing reunion. Charles very fit. Rehearsing new play. Love all relatives and friends.
Love Mum.

Guernsey 9.7.1943
Received no news from you this year. Are you alright? Everyone here OK. Think of you often. Be glad when this is all over,
Charles.

England 22.11.1943
Darling, had message from you today. Glad you have interest in theatricals. Also longing reunion. Cannot believe we have been married five years. Fondest love.

Guernsey 21.1.1944
Have no news from you for a year. Charles very disheartened. Are you well? We are all O.K.
Love all friends and relations. Mum.

Biberach, Germany 26.1.44
My dearest Kath and Dinkie we were so delighted to get your letter of July. You did not address it correct its been all over the place. Trying to trace us. You must write the print as well in the square on the other side. I am so pleased to send your dear mum and dad news of you, have just written them. Glad you are both well as we are. Many thanks dear for your kind offer. We have got such a lot of nice things from the Red Cross . We have told June not to send any more parcels. Have you had the news Peg got another boy, quite a little family with 4 babies, she must have her hands full, dear Peg. Will write as soon as I hear from your mum and dad. June told me in her last letter she had written you. Dears all our best love and hope to see you soon. God bless you dears and Baby Terry. Write soon
Uncle George & Auntie Ethel.

Guernsey 29.1.1944
No news of you eighteen months. Charles very disappointed. Behaving well. Still on stage. Had good Xmas altogether. Hoping see you shortly.
Muriel, Trav.

Guernsey 19.2.1944
Everyone here O.K. No news from you for 12 months. All spare time taken up with theatre, standard of entertainment high. Please write soon.
Love Charles.

Guernsey 26.2.1944
Dear Aunties, Longing to meet cousin Terry and Uncle George. See nannie everyday. Longing to see you all.
Love Cathleen, Michael, Maureen, Brian.

Biberach, Germany 8.3.44
Dear Kathie and Dinkie, mum delighted news of you. Mary Carberry died February, sad. My Darlings so pleased to get your letter, had no news from you for a year. Charlie comes round quite often and was thrilled to read the letter he asked me to send you all his love, to say he misses you very much. He is working at the old place, doing very well in amateur plays. Maurice is working at the Piette. Daddie is resting. Very sorry to hear about Bob, did not know. Give our love to Auntie Lil, thank her very much from us for being so kind to you. I knew she would be. Bless her Peg has had 4 babies in 4 years all lovely. They keep us busy. Fancy Dink with a baby of her own, how I would love to see him. Give him a big hug and kisses from us all. Is George staying with you or is he in the services? Write as much as you can. God Bless and keep you safe. Fondest love from us all Mum, Dad, Charlie, Peg, Maurice. Got a snap of Charlie cannot send it to you will keep it for when I see you.
Love Aunt Ethel.

Guernsey 24.3.1944
Thrilled with recent news via Ethel. Please continue that way. Uncle
Emile died two weeks ago, long illness. Looking forward to reunion.
Keep smiling. Charles.

Guernsey 29.4.1944
Keeping fit. Started sunning, swimming soon. Drank your health
sixth anniversary. Hope with you next. Both families well. Still on
stage.
All my love. Charles.

Guernsey 26.5.1944
Hope you are O.K. Am brown as a berry, plenty of bathing. Taking
holidays in June. Keep your end up. Doing same here.
Love Charles.

After the Normandy landings on the 6th June 1944, the Channel
Islands became cut off from the rest of the world. There were no
further messages.

I sat for a long while. Stunned. The 1940s held me, refusing
to let me go. Unsynchronised and lacking in substance, the
letters read like a dysfunctional social media thread. Yet to me
they conveyed a powerful message. Beneath the words lay the
reality of my parent's separation; the cold, dark, emptiness of it.

I caught a strong sense of my father from the few words
he sent my mother each month. Loving and steady, just as I
remembered him, and committed to getting his message across
within the parameters of the invisible rules. But her silhouette
seemed alien to me, enigmatically lingering on the edges of the
conversation, stepping in just occasionally and mostly to share
other people's news. Charles gently coaxing, Kath discreetly

hiding, as their words danced back and forth across the gulf that divided them. Does she laugh or does she cry? It is impossible to tell, but one thing is certain; her long periods of silence are deafening.

I reflected on the diverging lives from which these letters came. As Mum's horizons were widening to the vastness of the English countryside and the wartime possibilities for women, Dad's were constricting daily under Nazi oppression. The beaches he liked to visit, the cliff paths he enjoyed walking, all gradually becoming out of bounds. And, while she embraced the new experience of living in a large town, making new friends and feeling valued for her contribution to the war effort, he lived in the same house, continued in the same job and grew close to the small group of friends that remained.

Meanwhile, the news of those all around them thrived on the birth of the wartime babies. Benign, uncontroversial news; at least on the surface.

Auntie Peg 4: Auntie Dink 1: Mum 0.

Whatever details lay buried in her wartime experience, it is clear that Mum faced her second illegitimate pregnancy with a very different mindset from the first. With the war likely to end soon, and the mood of the country much more optimistic, her mood had significantly changed too. Society would still have waved its disapproving finger at her, but giving a healthy baby up for adoption must have been every bit as painful as losing Michael, and no amount of disapprobation could have persuaded her to give another baby away to such an irrevocable process. This time she chose a different path for her daughter, a path that would leave her options open. She allowed herself the luxury of giving her daughter a name, Michele, before placing her in the care of St Christopher's Children's Home in Hinton Martell. She still needed to return to Bridgwater to work, but at least now she would be able to visit her baby whenever she wanted.

Over a third of the babies born in Britain during World War 2 were illegitimate, and by the end of the war, two out of every three petitions for adultery were being filed by men. Anxiety and separation had proved unbearable for many wives and their loneliness had led to an epidemic of wartime adultery. Nevertheless, society found their plight unworthy of compassion. In the wake of the deaths of tens of millions of people, the survivors of the wartime generation were considered the lucky ones, whatever the depths of their own personal tragedies.

When the war ended Charles would be the first to write, desperate to reconnect with his wife, longing to share his experience. What Kath felt we can only speculate.

My eyes lingered over the last item in my pile of wartime correspondence. Sent ten days after Guernsey was liberated by the allies, it was a telegram:

GUERNSEY 19TH MAY 1945
IS ANYTHING WRONG. NO NEWS. VERY WORRIED.
LOVE MUM DAD LOVERIDGE

CHAPTER 2

The Second Baby

MY SEARCH THROUGH THE first box, though fascinating, had not proved as fruitful as I had first anticipated. But I still had two boxes to go. Pete had left me to it and when I searched him out to ask if he could fetch me another box from the attic he seemed surprised that I should be asking for a second so quickly after opening the first. Had I perhaps been a bit hasty in my search? Was I certain I hadn't missed anything? What had I found? Nevertheless, he did as requested and went back up to the attic whilst I returned to our garden room to clear the decks for a new search.

"There you go!" Pete said with a flourish, as he sliced open the tape before relaxing back onto the sofa next to me. This time, it seemed, he was not going to leave me to it.

"Thank you!" I said, opening up the flaps and wondering, momentarily, if he was staying to ensure that my search through the second box would be sufficiently thorough.

To my delight, the box was brimming with all manner of memorabilia; trophies of past lives that, like virgin territory, had remained largely undiscovered until now. Halfway through my search I came upon a medium-sized rosewood jewellery casket. I lifted it out of the box, sat back, and tentatively opened the lid which was lined with an exquisite quilting of sky-blue satin. A wooden tray, painted in matt silver, and containing various trinkets, floated on top of a bundle of theatre programmes and newspaper cuttings. Placing the box to one side, Pete and I settled down to look through them. Dad, it seemed, had achieved some success as an actor. The reviews were mostly positive and he had enjoyed a starring role in several of the productions.

I replaced the programmes and was just about to close the lid when I noticed a tiny silver clasp at the top of the quilted lining. Releasing the clasp released the lining and three small, pastel blue, envelopes and a postcard fell out! Each envelope was bulging under the strain of its tightly folded contents; one addressed in my father's handwriting and two in my mother's. Tucked between them was a small postcard in my father's handwriting. The dates, though faded, were sufficiently legible to enable me to place them in chronological order. First was the card, with the official heading "Reoccupation of Channel Islands."

May 15th 1945

Dear Kath,

Well darling here's a week gone already and what a week for us. Things are certainly moving and we are all looking forward to our first issue of rations sometime this week.

Everyone here O.K. and the home still intact. Expecting mail from you, so please write often.

Love Charles

This, I assumed, must be Dad's second message to Mum after the end of the war. She had kept his first letter separately, in a vanity case under her side of the bed, and I had read it many times. But this one I had never seen. I had yet to find her first letter to him. I couldn't help thinking that she might not have been as eager to write to him as he had been to write to her.

I passed the card to Pete and slid the first of the letters carefully out of its envelope and gently smoothed out the folds.

Romo
21st May 1945

My Darling Kath,

What a joy to receive news at last. I have just finished work, and couldn't get home quickly enough, as Peg phoned me and told me that she had had a letter from you and that possibly there would be one for me. Well, there were two, and the cigs many thanks for them darling, they are just what the doctor ordered. We had a free gift of 50 over the weekend, though we can't as yet buy any until the shops are stocked again.

Well darling there is so much to tell you that I don't quite know where to start. Anyway there's one thing, the Hun never got us down, in fact on many occasions we had the laugh of him, robbing him wherever possible.

You're not the only one, darling, who has put on weight, I have put on a stone in four years, but don't ask me how, mostly on potatoes and parsnips, when we could get them. The younger people here have stuck it fairly well, but the older people have lost a terrible lot, three, four and five stone in most cases, due not only to short rations, but to constant worry.

Our rations have been scanty and very monotonous, the vegetable bill taking the place of the pre-war grocery bill. Our rations in the good parts of the year being as nearly as I can tell you; Bread; Male 6lbs and female 4lbs per week, a 2lb loaf being about the size of a 1lb pre-war loaf and of very inferior quality. 2ozs sugar, sometimes a little flour, and 3ozs butter per week, skimmed milk for five years, and 5lbs potatoes for eight months of the year and whatever we could scrounge or buy on the black market.

We were always hungry, especially in cold weather, though we had enough to exist on, and at Christmas and holiday times we always continued to have a good feast. If it had not been for the black market we should all have starved, but what a price we had to pay! From Christmas 1944 until V day we had no rations from the Germans, living almost entirely on Red Cross parcels and, "joy of joys", white bread, cabbage leaves and potato peels.

Muriel and Trav have been wonderfully good to us, giving us little extras and tips on where to get things. Trav had his bar open and therefore had dealings with people in the know, and we have spent every Christmas with them. Do you remember Mr Travers! How he made you laugh so much when Muriel got married! He's always the same and we have had some grand times with him.

Well, darling, I must tell you a bit about myself. First of all, as you know, I never worried about anything just taking things as they came. Well I've carried on like that. I always had a feeling that you were well looked after, though I was disappointed at not getting much news and, knowing that, I hadn't a care in the world about Jerry or anyone else, you see we knew we would win this war.

I went in for amateur theatricals, starting in musical comedy and then turning to drama etc and that will be my hobby after things have settled once more, plays etc being banned since D Day on account of lack of electricity.

Then I learned to play a piano, by ear only, and though not good can knock up a tune anywhere any time. After that I was complimented on my swimming, being always on the beach in the summer and brown as a berry, a fact which contributed in no small manner to my general fitness, though twice in 1943 I had a very bad spell with my gums, being under the dentist for a long time and having my gums burnt several times, a pretty drastic cure but the only one, due to lack of vitamins i.e. oranges and lemons etc.

Then, in November last until March this year, I was under the doctor for blood poisoning and skin trouble coming out in sores which gave me hell in bed, nearly driving me mad with itching, this also from lack of certain foods, though in neither case was I laid up but went on as usual, the only effect being an uncomfortable feeling.

However, I am okay again and have a good tan, having started bathing in March.

I have played a lot of table tennis this winter and done well, also from March until V Day I have been floor manager of a small roller skating rink at Saumarez Park where I earned from £2 to £3 per week which went on black market stuff.

Now Betty has got a type writer, Bill having pinched it from a Hun last week, so I am having a go at that now.

I am still in the same job, and have been having an easy spell, as since February the civilians have had no current and we have only been running from 9am to 4pm. Though someone had to be there. For three years we had our wages reduced, in my case by £1 a week and, though I had the rents reduced, it is still fairly stiff and what with that and the cost of living it has been a job to make ends meet.

However darling, I have kept our home intact and I still have the radio, having cunningly hidden it when they were called in by the Germans in 1942, and when, in November 1944, they had me for pinching oil (for cooking, gas being severely rationed) the Gestapo searched the house for a crystal set at the same time, they were within a foot of the radio and didn't know it. Incidentally we had three crystal sets at that time one of them being in Bill's mac pocket in the hall when the Gestapo were there! For that affair I was fined 50rm that is about £5 5d, or 10 days, being the lightest fine of the eight of us that were caught, the others being a little scared and admitting too much. We had no trial, just making a statement to Gestapo HQ, singly of course, and a week later being notified of sentence, some of the chaps being fined from £10 to £50.

Another thing I have learned is to speak a fair amount of German, and if I had started earlier I should now be able to speak it fluently. Until D Day we had no guards or Germans on the works, but from then on we always had a Hun on duty, and speaking with them I picked up quite a lot, very often acting as a kind of interpreter, unofficially of course, between them and our chaps at work, and recently between prisoners working in the works and our own "Tommies".

Well darling, I am glad you kept my suit as I need it pretty badly. I have only had one pair of pants now in five years. Do you remember the sports coat you gave me in 1936! Well I had that dyed brown three years ago, after having worn it at work for a long time. I also have my black suit, but the coat is long since too small. As to underwear, well that is a problem I hope to rectify in the near future.

I cannot send you a snap as I haven't had one taken since you went, films here being scarce and cameras forbidden, but please send me some of you.

Well my darling, I must close now though I still feel that I have forgotten something. Give my kindest regards to Mrs Finch and friends, love to Dink and junior, and please write soon.

With all my love

Charles

Xxxxxxxxxxxxxxxxx

P.S. Excuse scribble am feeling drowsy was up at 5:30am this morning.

"Wow," I exclaimed softly to myself, immersed in thought, dazed by Dad's words.

"Can I read it?" Pete interrupted, respectful of my right to read it first but impatient, now, to seize his chance. With a jolt, I remembered I was not alone.

"Of course," I said, mindlessly passing him the letter, still absorbed in its contents.

My parents had been happily married before the war, but it felt almost as if they had found themselves courting again. I knew that Dad had received far fewer Red Cross letters from Mum than she had from him, but this did not seem to have deterred him. He had been the first to write and for her, that must have been very encouraging.

My mind drifted back to the early spring of 1945 as I tried to imagine what Mum might have been thinking as she tentatively reached out to her husband after five years apart. The man behind the words she was receiving was very much the husband she remembered, so she must have felt a glimmer of hope that forgiveness could be found if she reached for it gently.

She mustn't be too quick to tell him things that she knew he wouldn't want to hear; but time was on her side, at least in that moment. She could appeal to the actor in him, setting out her scenes carefully and taking her cues from him. And, as the long years of their separation slowly melted away, as inevitably they must, she would bide her time and allow fate to arrive at its verdict.

11 Kidsbury Road
Bridgwater
Saturday 9th June 1945

My darling husband,

Received your letter this morning, what a lovely long commentary on your activities as an actor. I'm glad, darling, that you had something to occupy your mind. I will keep the photo safely. I recognised one of the Gardner boys, and Marjorie Falla, but the other faces seem strange, should I know them? And which one played opposite you?

Yes, darling, I have seen a few rather good plays although never bothered to go to anything in Bridgwater, but have been to Bristol a few times where they get all the top liners from time to time. I saw Robert Morley in a marvellous one "the man who came to dinner". Exactly like the film in which Bettie Davis and Monty Woolley starred.

Well, darling, today has been my Saturday off and I've been

scouting around for parts for your bike and I believe I will be able to get a tyre and inner tube shortly. The man in the shop is expecting some in and he hopes to fix me up. It must be very difficult I know for you. As I told you I have a little bike, a utility one, black of course with white mudguards and I've already had to have one new tyre. I had a puncture a short while ago. I had a collision in the town with some dumb chuck, who was cycling on the wrong side of the road. But Bill and Norman, between them fixed it up for me, and as a matter of fact I have a new inner tube in the garage at the moment, but it won't be any good for your bike.

I don't know quite what to do whether to sell my bike or not. Shall I hang onto it and have it sent on later? It's quite a nice little bike, very light and has been useful to hop around on.

I have done an awful lot of knitting these past years, and was wondering if you would like me to make you some socks and a pullover, I could raise a few coupons for that. Do you like hand knitted socks? Lily has made dozens of pairs (sorry darling will have to continue in pencil hardly a drain of ink in the bottle) of utility socks that they make now, only cover the ankles.

I wonder what you are doing now? It's just about 8 o'clock and music hall is coming on just now, on the wireless. Finchy and Bill are back, thank goodness, I haven't half been lonely in the house by myself.

Darling you said in your letter for me to write and tell the folks about the second baby but it's such a lot to explain and I don't want to upset them. I thought if I told them all about it when I saw them I could explain it much better. Have you any reason why I should? If you want to, you could tell them, and say I didn't want to upset them as it all happened so long ago.

Well my darling, write soon and tell me all the news, and exactly what you are doing now? Also is there any definite news yet as to our possible return, let me know as soon as you can so that I can act accordingly.

Enclosing a couple more packets of cig. papers. Hope by now you have received the cigs okay that I sent. I'm leaving your suit a while yet, as they say at the GPO that it's still doubtful as to the certainty of it arriving okay and as I've had it for five years it won't hurt a while longer.

Well my darling I think that's all for this time.

Lots of love as ever

Your wife

Kath

xxxxxxxxxxxxxxxxx

I read the letter through twice. The tiny clue had been subtly woven into the fabric of the letter, designed to be overlooked by the casual observer. This was what I had been searching for, yet it answered nothing. Who was the 'second baby'? Michele? Pauline? The stillbirth? There were no other clues and all I had found were more questions. I was exhausted from the emotional rollercoaster that had taken control of my life; but I couldn't disembark from it, not even for a moment.

'What a wonderful letter" Pete said, his eyes shining as he passed me back Dad's letter.

"You wait till you read this one!" I whispered, passing him Mum's letter but refusing to meet his eyes. I didn't want him to question me, I wanted to find out what he would make of it himself.

Meanwhile, I had one letter left.

Tuesday, June 19, 1945

My darling husband,

I really should be working but honestly I don't feel like it. It's the most marvellous day. Sun blazing down, it seems such a sin to be stuck in this office, no one feels like work this weather.

I wonder what you are doing now it's 2.20pm and I have just come back from dinner. If I was home I would like nothing more than to be by the sea.

I would love to see you buying your clothes. Now darling for heaven sake go careful with your coupons, I know you will feel very well off with coupons but honestly darling, go very careful with them and buy as good clothes as you possibly can. We may be on clothes rations for ages yet. The first year we all went a bit mad with our coupons but soon got down to making the best of them.

This is your celebration week isn't it? I went to the pictures last night and saw the newsreel of the King and Queen but it was very short and we couldn't recognise any people.

We still haven't had a reply yet about coming home, although some Guernsey people here have heard. I was wondering if it would be a good idea to send some of my things back by post. I have a few books I have collected. Let me know what you think.

Also darling let me know what you have got in the clothing line as George can get me some things for you when he goes back to Ireland. Also let me know size etc he asked me on Saturday if I would like some shirts for you. I think he can get most things like that, vests, pyjamas etc but I don't want to get things that you already have as you know things are difficult to get, on the other hand I feel you must be stocked in clothes or we should only have to get them later on.

Well my darling, I haven't cigarette papers to put in this letter but will send off a few cigs tomorrow. I expect there will be a letter from you tomorrow, there usually is on Wednesdays. I keep getting the old snaps out and having another look at you. Gosh I feel more excited than before we were married.

I got weighed yesterday, nine stone four, I have lost a few pounds. I think it's all the excitement. Finchie thinks you look awfully nice. Don't worry darling, they will be over to see us as soon as they can.

Jack Okie was in the picture last night he is one of your old favourites isn't he? He is terribly fat but still a good trooper. Spencer Tracy seems to be better than ever, he was good in a film we saw the other day, "A guy named Joe".

I've got stacks of mending to do tonight, I think if it's like this I will take it out in the garden to do.

George has made Dink a fine wireless, he bought it all the way from Ireland. He is looking forward to coming over to see us all.

There seems to be crowds of people not coming back. Some of them have got such good jobs over here. I wish I could bring mine over with me. I seem to be getting on so well here now. But I wouldn't swap it for my life with you. Although the extra money would've done us some good.

Do write and tell me all you do this week as I am very interested. I expect everyone will be very gay. I'm longing to get back to see my home again, can't remember what it was like.

Well my darling, the old man is in the distance so afraid I must pack up.

Till next time au revoir.

All my love darling

xxxxxxxxx Your Kath xxxxxxxxx

What a privilege it felt to be given this intimate insight into the lives of a young couple, now in their late twenties, as they caught up on five extraordinary years apart. I passed Pete the final letter and sat back to try to process what I had read.

"Well? What do you think?" I asked when he had finally finished reading all the letters.

"I don't know what to think," he replied, unsure what to say, reluctant to pass judgement. It was not often that Pete was lost for words.

"Who do you think she was referring to when she mentioned the 'second baby'"? I persisted.

"Michele!" he sounded definite.

"But she says 'it all happened so long ago' and Michele was born just 5 months before she wrote that letter?"

Pete fell silent, he hadn't scrutinised the detail or analysed it in the way I had. He shrugged. "Must have been Pauline then?"

"Maybe. But it could have been the stillbirth," I offered, "though I don't understand why that would be 'such a lot to explain'"?

"Perhaps there are more letters," he said hopefully, but somehow I doubted it. It was with their blessing that I was reading these, I knew that now. Dad had left them for me, knowing that, in time, I would find them and be interested. The references to other letters, however, I found deeply concerning. It was possible that there were more to be found, packed away somewhere, but there was an order to this second box that suggested some form of censorship.

Before Dad left his home for the very last time, when his health was failing and we had invited him to come to live with us, he asked one of my cousins, who did odd jobs for him around the house and garden, to burn a whole load of paperwork.

CHAPTER 3

Empty Cases

ALL THE OUTWARD SIGNS, at least as I remember them, were that my parents lived straightforward lives in their bungalow on the outskirts of Town. Their food cupboards contained just enough of everything to last them until the next weekly shop. The shelves in their lounge celebrated modest, happy lives with understated displays of holiday souvenirs, wedding presents and gifts from me as I was growing up. There was no excess, no clutter, just a calm and well-ordered home from which they could live their lives of routine. The contents of their attic, however, were telling a very different story.

In the final box, I found further evidence of hoarders, of people who knew the significance of their past and were reluctant to throw any of it away. It was packed full of different-sized containers that Pete had seemingly arranged according to some best-fit algorithm. The tiny treasure chests eagerly offered themselves up for inspection, as if privacy had somehow wearied them and they were grateful for the release. Scattered within them were fragments of information that, when pieced together, painted a fascinating insight into the lives of those who had placed them there. I was glad that I hadn't dealt with it all sooner. Here lay a wealth of material to compensate for all those years of neglect, had I looked through it earlier I might easily have discarded vital clues.

With the opening of each container came a sense of oxygen, pumping into lives that had lain dormant for years, as my parents' past started to explode into life. Trawling through the minutiae of their lives I found utility bills, travel tickets, notebooks, Income Tax demands, Christmas cards, bank statements ... all the footprints of people who had walked through pre-digital times. I began to emotionally connect with their lives and, to my surprise, I found they had led lives very similar to my own. They had bank accounts to balance, holidays to plan, friends to keep in contact with. But the unique period of history through which they had travelled gave a texture to their lives that I had never fully appreciated until now.

As I dug deeper into the woman my mother had been, I needed to keep my own feelings in check and take care not to project them onto her. I was a mother myself, and I found her experience of motherhood heartbreaking, but she and I were different people, playing out our lives in very different times. If she could live her life, with a smile on her face, and without burdening others with the weight of her grief, then I owed it to her to at least try to do the same. It was easy to focus on the enormity of her loss, but in so doing I risked undervaluing the woman that she became and the purpose of her life. In any case, there was plenty of evidence that pointed towards happier times and that deserved due consideration too.

In an old envelope, I found two black and white photographs of people I didn't recognise. The first was an official army photograph of a soldier on which was recorded a name and a number in my mother's handwriting.

39383 E Woodward. Sick.

The man was young and handsome, with a lazy left eye and a shy smile. An ordinary-looking guy, with the slight aura of pride that suggested he was about to start playing his part. Could this be the father of one, or maybe both, my sisters?

The second was a photograph of a young woman in her twenties:

> To Kath,
> In loving memory of our war effort
> at British Cellophane.
> Bridgwater chemicals
> Empty cases etc.
> Good Luck & Best Wishes
> Eileen 26.6.45

I studied their faces for a very long time; first one, then the other, then back to the first. I had an album somewhere that Dad had put together of photos from around the same era. I recalled a couple of mum with her friends in Bridgwater and another of the people she had lived with. But I had never seen any that felt as personal to her as these.

These must be people who had played a crucial role in her life; people she had cared enough about to keep their photographs safe. Perhaps it might be possible to trace them? I posted the photographs on research websites, social media platforms and in the Bridgwater Mercury newspaper. They attracted little more than a casual passing interest.

The Rifles Museum was able to identify the soldier as belonging to the senior (129th) infantry brigade of the 43rd Wessex Division of the 4th battalion of the Somerset Light Infantry. This meant little to me, but I was interested in their suggested date for the photo, 1942, because that was the year that Pauline was born.

———

My search through the removals boxes had been fascinating but it had raised more questions than it had provided answers. As I packed my treasures back into their dusty tombs I asked Pete to find a place to store them that was more readily accessible to me than the attic. I knew that I would find myself returning to the boxes in the near future, but for now, I needed to look elsewhere for clues.

To date, I had shared my story with just a handful of people. It wasn't that I wanted to keep it secret, nor that I was ashamed of it in any way, it was simply that I considered it too precious an offering to gift to the casual observer. Well-meaning people would sometimes suggest how I might be feeling, but the wisest of them did not attempt such intimacy. Empathy could never be in anyone's gift because my experience was unique, and I certainly did not welcome sympathy. I alone held the rights to my story and the colours at its centre were truer than ever, it was only around the edges that the image had begun to blur.

It was around this time that I started to write. For a trained maths teacher this took me well out of my comfort zone, but I found putting pen to paper cathartic, at least at first. It gave me the time, the space and the medium in which to examine and express how I was feeling. Very soon, however, the sense of responsibility in the telling of a story which was not wholly mine to tell began to weigh heavily. Accuracy was essential, yet I hadn't the slightest idea how to successfully address all the unanswered questions and gaps in my understanding. It was crucial that I continue my research to try to solve as much of the mystery as possible.

I borrowed Auntie Dink's address book from Val and wrote to each Bridgwater address, introducing myself as Dink's niece, and requesting contact. It was certainly possible that there were people still living in Bridgwater that might remember Mum. I did get a couple of replies, from people keen to share their own memories of the past, but none of them could remember her. Then one day the phone rang.

"Hello, am I speaking to Jackie?" The voice sounded old, but not frail.

"Hello? Yes, this is Jackie?"

"I'm phoning about the letter you sent me? My name is Margaret and I knew of your Mum when she lived in Bridgwater during the war …"

My heart thumped so loudly that I was afraid she might hear it; the call had caught me off guard.

"Hello Margaret! Thank you very much for phoning," I managed, trying to steady my nerves so that I might properly welcome her call.

"I didn't know her well," she continued quickly as if she were afraid of giving me false hope, "because I was just a child at the time. But your mum's sister, Dink, was friendly with my older sister, Helen, so she was often at our house."

"You're the first person I've spoken to who actually knew of Mum during the war," I said, in an attempt to steer the conversation through neutral territory whilst my mind raced ahead, searching for the best way to introduce my query. "It must have been very tough on her as an evacuee, I wish I'd asked her more about it but I'm ashamed to say I was never really interested."

"She's no longer alive then." She stated it simply, and I detected disappointment, and a hint of sadness in her tone, that I should have been better prepared for.

"She sadly passed away many years ago," I said quietly, "and all I know about her life during the war is that she lived in Bridgwater and that she worked in a gunpowder factory!"

"Yes! She worked at British Cellophane," Margaret

interjected, "and they did make munitions for the war. So ... why the interest now?"

"Well ... I found out something about her recently that was a bit of a shock ... not in a bad way at all ... just something I had never known ..." I hesitated, hoping she might help me out, but Margaret remained silent, presumably waiting for me to continue. I wondered how much I should tell her. I had no wish to upset this elderly lady who had kindly taken the trouble to phone me. But I had come this far, it was surely a risk worth taking? I took a deep breath. "I found out that Mum had two babies during the war that I knew nothing about ..."

Still Margaret remained silent. Perhaps she also knew nothing? Or perhaps she just needed reassurance as to my motives before opening herself up to me.

"I don't have a problem with it at all," I added hastily, "and I don't have any bad thoughts about her or anything. I've managed to trace both my sisters and it's wonderful to have them in my life. I would just like to find out what happened to Mum during the war ...". I broke off, I had laid my cards face-up on the table, it was up to her now. All I could do was hope that I hadn't said too much. It seemed an eternity before she spoke, and when she did she said the words so softly that they barely reached me.

"I knew about one baby."

"You did?" I whispered back. "Only one?"

"Only one. I overheard some talk about your mum and a baby in our kitchen one day ..."

And with that, Margaret took me back to the 1940s to sit with her in the corner of the room, whilst she played with her toys and her mum and sister talked at the kitchen table about my mum and her unfortunate circumstances. But Margaret's memories of what was said were vague and innocent, the occasion remembered purely for its sense of secrecy and scandal.

She seemed slightly confused that I should be asking about two babies when she clearly only knew about one, and she seemed genuinely sorry that she couldn't help me any further, but she did have a suggestion as to what I might do next.

"Your Auntie Dink lived with Helen you know. If you give Helen a ring I know, for a fact, that she will be able to tell you everything."

"But I thought Mum and Dink lived together during the war?" I said, offering it as a question as I had no wish to offend Margaret, though I felt certain she was wrong.

"For the first part of the war they did live together … with Lily in Kidsbury Road. But after Dink and your mum had their babies they fell out and that's when Dink moved in with Helen."

I took a sharp intake of breath. I had never thought to place the facts in order, to join the dots in my thinking. Dink's baby was born in January 1943 around the same time that Mum must have given her baby for adoption. They would have been pregnant at the same time! My throat tightened as I pictured Mum leaving Kidsbury Road, heavy with child and heavy with sadness at the long journey ahead and the loss that lay at the end of it. She would have returned just as Auntie Dink was bringing her baby home, surrounded by the love and support of Uncle George and his family. For a moment I felt defeated.

There was no welfare state to support Mum and no one to fall back on, she simply had to work. The best she could hope for was that a loving family would be found, a family that could offer her daughter the stable and happy upbringing that, given her current circumstances, Mum was unable to provide. The discovery that Mum and Dink had fallen out during this traumatic period in Mum's life was hard to comprehend.

"Hello? Jackie … are you still there? I hope I haven't upset you?"

"Yes, I'm still here Margaret. Sorry … I'm just trying to get my head around what you have just said. I had no idea that Mum and Auntie Dink fell out."

For a long while, neither of us spoke. I needed space to gather my thoughts but I was reluctant to let her go. She was a tangible connection with Mum's Bridgwater past, my only link to who she had been.

"You mustn't let it upset you, my dear. It was a long time ago and times are very different now." Her concern was genuine, Margaret was a kind lady.

"I'm really grateful to you for sharing this with me Margaret. Are you sure Helen would be happy for me to phone her?"

"Of course. Good luck. And please let me know how you get on."

I found Helen's number in Auntie Dink's address book, which meant I had written to her previously and she had not responded. I needed to be careful. Few people of her generation were as open-minded and honest about the past as Margaret. I applied the brakes to my impatience and took time to consider how best to introduce myself to Helen, how best to ask her about Mum. Yet, despite my measured approach, she raised her guard immediately and it was clear from the outset that she had no desire to speak to me. Perhaps I should have been more gently persuasive? But that's not my style. Disappointed, frustrated and a little stung by my failure, I too easily kowtowed to her wishes and allowed the call to leave me none the wiser.

The next day we agreed that Pete should phone her. His natural charm and politely persistent manner were certainly worth a try and, as predicted, she did prove a little more candid with him. Yes, she remembered Mum and yes, she did know of a baby, though it was a long time ago and she could remember no details. As Pete ended the call, he thanked her for talking to him and assured her of our continued gratitude if anything further should come to mind. And she agreed to phone us, if she thought of anything else, no matter how small or insignificant it might seem to her. The door had been left ajar and we felt confident that, given a little more time and patience, she might open it and invite us in.

Then, a few days later, I received the following letter from her …

5th June 2010

Dear Jackie,
Re: Kathleen Le Bargy & her sister Dink,

Both came over as refugees during the war. Kath stayed with Mrs Finch, Dink stayed with me.

I have no knowledge of babies & knowing Mrs Finch they would be kept quiet.

I also knew George Fletcher, who married Dink, he unfortunately died over here.

I have made enquiries but I seem to be then only one left that knew them round here. I am sorry I cannot help you.

Kindest regards,
Helen

It is just not possible to get some people to open their hearts. My mother alone held the rights to her story and had given no one permission to share it. As such, she could rest in peace, assured of the loyalty of a wartime generation that would no more betray her than recognise the hypocrisies of their cruel moral code. It was a generation that ranked duty above hopes and dreams, that drove her far from home to deliver her babies, and that tolerated her indiscretions only because she chose to leave them there. A generation that would reward her by locking the evidence away, not out of any misplaced sense of loyalty towards her, but because it could never hope to stand up to the scrutiny of their mutual shame.

Sometimes I just had to walk away.

CHAPTER 4

A Thousand Words

SOONER OR LATER THE wispy, entangled threads of enquiries that I had abandoned through frustration and despair, would call me back. Like Sirens calling to my soul, their allure was so powerful that I knew my escape from them could only ever be temporary. Even when it was clear that they could never carry the weight of my expectation, still their seduction was complete and my loyalty to them total.

As soon as I was able I visited Bridgwater, hoping to find evidence of Mum's story in the area she had lived and worked all those years earlier. On arrival, we headed straight for Kidsbury Road and Pete parked the car a respectful distance from number 11. A battalion of red brick houses stood, shoulder to shoulder, to our left, each one identifiable solely by its street number and armed with tightly fitting net curtains and tiny, concrete front yards. To our right, a mismatch of different-sized houses welcomed their visitors with gardens and trees and off-street parking. Number 11 stood to attention at the end of the red brick line.

Pete sensed I was wavering and gently, but firmly, urged me to go and knock on the door. As I got out of the car I felt the knot in my stomach tighten. It was here that Mum had lived during the most volatile and impressionable years of her life. She had walked these pavements, and cycled down this road, a countless number of times. I opened the wrought iron gate and entered the front yard of number 11. It was a dreary Sunday afternoon so there was a good chance I might find someone in. A lady opened the door, smiling and welcoming, and a little surprised at this intrusion into her weekend. We searched for ways in which she might help me but, in reality, too many years had passed. As I thanked her and made my way back to the car, I realised that I had held no expectation of finding answers in this house, I had merely wanted to see it for myself. I imagined Mum leaving the house pregnant and returning empty-handed. It was a pilgrimage I had made in her honour but I knew I would not come back again.

We spent three days in Bridgwater but found no mention of Mum anywhere other than a verification, in a book in one of the museums, that she had indeed lived at number 11 Kidsbury Road during the war. So it was back to Guernsey, to the memorabilia my parents had left, and the internet.

———

Again and again, I trawled through the removals boxes, each time uncovering tiny clues that I had missed in earlier searches. I learned that answers could be found on the tiniest scrap of paper, in the date on an envelope, or in the background of a picture. Many times the clues remained so firmly hidden that they only offered themselves up as relevant on my fourth, fifth or even sixth round of searching, and so I learned to throw nothing away.

Tucked inside a bundle of old holiday brochures of Bournemouth I found a photo of Mum and Dad strolling through Bournemouth gardens dated 5th October 1952 together with two business cards for accommodation in the area. Each was given "with compliments from Emma and Alice Rowan", and one had a 1954 calendar on the back. Evidence, perhaps, that my parents had visited Michele on more than one occasion in the decade after the war.

In an old cigar tin I found several official letters from as far afield as Sydney, Australia to London, England, spanning the early post-war years with a common theme running throughout.

Ministry of Labour and National Service,
8th October 1945

Dear Mr Le Bargy,

I have to refer to your letter of 23rd September 1945, addressed to the Headquarters of this Department, asking for information on vacancies in the electrical industries, and have to inform you that as long as you are in the Channel Islands we are unable, under present arrangements, to take steps to find you employment on the mainland.

Should you, however, still desire to come to the mainland for employment, you should, on arrival here, register for employment at a local office of the Ministry of Labour and National Service, when steps will be taken to find you suitable employment,

Yours faithfully,
W.F.C. White
For Regional Controller

Had I found these letters earlier I would have been astounded that the father I knew to be so devoted to his island home had, at one time, tried desperately to leave it. But now they made sense. It was not only Mum that would have faced condemnation from Guernsey society for her wartime indiscretions, Dad would equally have been scorned, had he openly accepted another man's child. Their only chance of raising Michele themselves was to build a new life elsewhere. They may have been unsuccessful, but they had at least tried to put things right, and that meant a lot to me.

I have stretched out my memory, for glimpses of Michele, until it is as thin as gossamer and threatens to burst under the weight of such scrutiny. But still, I remember very little about her. Val never found the photo she believed she had of Michele sitting on the wall and, eventually, I stopped asking her for it. My search through Dad's old photos had also drawn a blank. My parents, it seemed, had left no trace of her anywhere.

Then, one day, in an overlooked side compartment of an old wallet of my father's, I found two photographic slides. I held each one up to the light. It was difficult to make out any details other than that one was of a teenage girl leaning against a wall and the other was a photo of Mum, myself and the same girl. Each was dated June 1962. I took them into school and a colleague promised to digitalise them and email them to me when he could find the time. In a busy school such as ours, I knew that was unlikely to be soon. I would need to be patient.

I am sitting on the floor in the dining room at Romo. The woollen carpet is old and musty and needs to be swept. She is in the kitchen washing up; the connecting door between us closed. It is a quarter to two and the wireless is tuned in so that I can "listen with mother", except my mother is in the hallway, on the telephone to the grocery store. She is relaying our weekly shopping list because tomorrow is delivery day.

"This is the BBC for mothers and children at home." I am listening alone.

"Are you sitting comfortably? Then I'll begin ..." I am not sitting comfortably, I am restless and fidgeting, and waiting impatiently for her to finish her chores. I dare not go and disturb her in case she gets into trouble. We both know the rules. Only when she has finished her jobs is she allowed to come and play.

Daddy has promised we will show her around the island today. I wish she would hurry.

Suddenly the door bursts open. "I'm done!" she exclaims and I throw myself at her. "Put your cardie on," she tells me. "Hurry up … let's go!"

When I got home from school, later that same day, Pete was stood by the back door ready to intercept me. He had his hands held suspiciously behind his back and was beaming with excitement. This was unusual. He was normally out and about, or busy doing odd jobs in his garage, at this time of day.

"Sit down and close your eyes!" He commanded, edging around me so I couldn't see what he was hiding.

"Darling, what's going on?" I asked warily, Pete was not the frivolous type. Nevertheless, I sat down as requested and closed my eyes.

"These came for you and I thought you might like me to print them," he said, his voice suddenly choked with emotion. I opened my eyes as he placed two photographs in my hand. I took a few moments to try to understand the first image. I didn't recognise the teenage girl, though there was something about her that seemed vaguely familiar. But when I saw her in the second photo the vague familiarity became much more tangible.

"What do you think?" he asked, searching my eyes for clues as to how I might be feeling.

But he had already lost me to the summer of 1962 and the magic of that moment.

Our shadows mingle, a huddle of three, as we do as directed and look straight at the camera, squinting into the sharpness of the early summer sun. We stand close, but not touching, halfway along the dam of Guernsey's main reservoir, waiting patiently for Dad to capture the significance of the moment. Above the drab greyness of the walkway lies the vintage green of the Guernsey countryside beneath a long-since faded sky. The concrete and the abstract preserved in time.

The two of them stand behind me wearing pastel knitted cardigans in yellow and blue, tightly buttoned over knee-length cotton dresses. Their hair is dark brown, wavy and gloriously thick, with partings that fall naturally to the left. Rosy cheeks paint the same faces, thirty years apart; a harmony of nature and nurture binding them together. But their smiles feel touchy and partial, as if they have yet to develop a certainty between them as she leans back on the thick grey wall behind her, relaxed and easy, whilst Mum stands beside her, daring to hope.

It is me who is the odd one out. Standing in front with my pink cardigan unbuttoned and a face that's been painted by a very different brush. My skin is pale and freckled and my fine, blonde hair has been swept back into a tight ponytail at the back of my head.

The two of them standing together. Whilst I am alone, left clutching my doll.

I was certain. It must be her.

I looked back at the first photo of Michele, leaning up against the wall. She was smiling happily at the camera, full of hope at being given her own stage; her own moment in time. Tragic when you knew the outcome.

Finally, I had found the treasure I had been seeking. Tangible evidence that, a long time ago, Michele spent time with us; that we were briefly a family.

When I sent the photos to Sharon and Charley, they were certain too and, overcome with emotion, they thanked me, many times over. The photos were equally important to them because they were the only ones they had ever seen of Michele when she was young.

'A picture is worth a thousand words,' and we had two.

CHAPTER 5

Sisters

IN SPITE OF MY obsession with understanding the past, I considered it far more important to nurture my relationships with my new families. Finding I had two sisters relatively late in life meant everything to me, and thankfully each seemed equally invested in our joint future. Love was our gift and we gave it freely, choosing to celebrate what we had found rather than commiserate over our loss. As the days turned into weeks and the weeks into years, the equilibrium of our lives was gently restored and my new families became very much part of my ordinary everyday.

Whenever possible I saw each of them on my occasional trips to the mainland and, in between visits, we spoke as regularly as our busy lives would allow. Each was interested in the stories I shared of the other and I hoped that, in time, they might come to speak directly rather than through me.

Pauline and Ken made their first visit to Guernsey in 2012 and gave me free rein to introduce them to all that Guernsey had to offer. I knew that they were keen birdwatchers and that they enjoyed walking, so Guernsey naturally ticked many of the boxes on their holiday wish list. But they also came to meet their extended family, to get to know our friends and to thank Patricia for bringing us together.

Throughout their stay, Pauline continued to share information with me about her experiences growing up. Her adoptive family had endured more than its fair share of problems, but this did not seem to have wearied her. She maintained a quietly determined, yet compassionate, outlook on life. Her fascination with our story was undoubtedly genuine and, to my considerable relief, she talked frequently and openly about our mother whilst appearing to hold no grudge against her. However, she expressed this interest in a more detached, less emotional way than me, and she appeared to have little appetite for trying to uncover the skeletons that lay buried in our family closet.

Michele took little persuasion to visit, and I loved having her to stay, but she hated travelling and would only come if her partner, or one of her family, accompanied her. On one occasion we brought her back with us on our return from a holiday abroad which gave us plenty of quality time to spend together. It was the year after my first contact with Pauline and, though I had spoken freely and often about each sister to the other, they had not yet spoken.

One day I suggested to Michele that we might phone Pauline together so that she could "meet" her for the first time. I expected her to withdraw a little, just as she had done when her family first contacted me. To my surprise, she was keen to phone straight away and from that first call, it was clear that they would get on well. Their circumstances had perhaps given them more in common with each other than either of them had with me, and I was pleased to see their friendship develop and our sisterhood flourish. For some reason, that I never fully understood, they held back from meeting each other in person. Instead, they chose to speak regularly on the phone, secure in the comfort of the mutually respectful bond they were gradually creating. It was as if the three of us had agreed, without uttering a word, to enjoy our own small miracle while we could. We knew that nothing lasts forever and we had little appetite for regret.

When Michele visited I needed to be mindful that, in many respects, she looked upon Guernsey as her home and already knew it quite well. So I continued to hold back from promoting my own agenda and instead let her determine what she would like to do. This was particularly important when she brought members of her family with her, as she was understandably keen to introduce Guernsey to them as her island. On one occasion she and Sharon made an unexpected visit for my birthday. I am not an easy person to surprise, but on this occasion, I genuinely had no idea they were coming. Anneka collected them from the airport and brought them straight to the restaurant where I was enjoying a celebratory meal with friends; it was the best birthday present I have ever had.

Whether she came with family or on her own, however, Michele remained wary of entering into any dialogue that involved reflecting on her past. I did try, when the mood seemed appropriate, to gently coax her to share a few memories, but mostly I was unsuccessful. Until one day, when we were sitting having a cup of tea and she seemed relaxed and happy, I asked her why she so despised our mother.

"Because she kept taking me back Bubba. She kept taking me back."

That was as far as she ever went and I had to respect the fact that the past was a road that she did not want to go back down. Though she stopped short of actually saying it, she believed that life had cheated her, and I believed it wise to count myself lucky that at least she didn't blame me.

CHAPTER 6

Sally

CHARLEY WAS THE ONLY person as proactive in her quest for the truth as I was. Her quick wit brought a whole new perspective to the search, opening up lines of enquiry that often proved challenging to pursue. Having been the one to initiate contact she felt an ongoing responsibility towards me, but she was also close to Michele, and therefore sometimes resisted following up on leads in case we discovered something that might upset her. I felt the same about my mum so I left Charley room to pull back whenever she needed to. In any case, we each had our own lives to lead and we couldn't spend all our time chasing shadows from the past.

I posted Mum and Michele's story on several internet forums and it attracted a moderate amount of interest. Most people could offer little more than random, anecdotal snapshots on the edges of their lives:

Dear Jag,

I was born in 1942 but I was at St Christopher's for the holidays until I was 13 or 14. Your mum's name is very familiar to me. I believe that she had a rather lovely head of mid-brown hair and rosy cheeks ...

Joan

And then on 21st January 2011 I received the following email:

Hi Jag,

I understand you wish to contact anyone that knew Michele – well I was brought up with her at St Christopher's Children's Home – for info that may be of use to you please contact me if you wish.

Regards Sally

After so many disappointments I could hardly believe my luck! This was the Sally who had been Michele's best friend at school, the lady Sharon had told me about; the lady with the baby. I replied at once, and she must have been expecting it because she replied immediately, too, inviting me to give her a call.

"Hi, Sally! It's Jag! Thank you so much for contacting me. You have no idea how pleased I am to hear from you ..." I could feel myself rushing, I needed to slow down. I didn't want to scare her off as I had Helen.

"I emailed you as soon as I heard about the message you posted online." She sounded just as eager. "Have you heard from anyone else that was at St Christopher's?"

"Not really, no one that actually knew Michele," I said a little more calmly. It was okay to be excited, just not too excited. "And you must have known her especially well ..."

"I don't think anyone knew her better than me!" she interrupted with an air of pride. "There were only three full-time residents at St Christopher's when we were there, Michele, myself and a boy called Peter. The other children were all there on a temporary basis. So the three of us did everything together. We had a very happy upbringing, you know, and I have so many wonderful memories ..." She paused, suddenly uncertain. "Is there anything in particular you would like to know?"

Finally! Here was a witness to Michele's childhood who, I sensed, might be willing to share their collective past with me. But I had not, as yet, given her any idea who I was or the reason for my sudden interest. If I wanted her to speak openly and honestly to me I needed to lead by example. So I told her a little bit about myself, about Charley's first email and the ways in which it had changed my life. Whether I was giving her enough information, or perhaps too much, I had no way of knowing because she listened, without interrupting, until I fell silent.

"Wow!" she said finally, and with a hint of disbelief. "You never knew about her?"

"No. I had no idea."

"I can't believe they never told you," she said wistfully; sad for me, sad for her friend.

"I'm pretty sure they tried," I offered, not wanting her to think ill of my parents. " I remember Dad told me once about a girl who ran away from our family. I got so upset at the thought of someone running away from us that he never mentioned it again. And I remember a young girl coming to work for Mum in our guest house one year, and that it felt a bit like having a sister."

"That would definitely have been her!" Sally confirmed. "She was sent to Guernsey when she was 17. Up until then, we had seldom been apart and I really missed her when she left."

As Sally shared her experiences of the schools she and Michele had gone to, the Christmases and birthdays they had celebrated, and the lives they had led, I reflected on the depth of their relationship. They were sisters, if not in blood then definitely in spirit, and I began to feel a little uncomfortable referring to myself as Michele's sister when I had such a flimsy claim to the title.

"We were always together," she ended, simply.

"When did you last see her?" I asked, not wanting her to stop. It was fascinating to feel Michele's past bursting into life. She was no longer the mysterious figure weaving its way in and out of my world. She was a little girl growing up alongside other children, doing all the normal things that children do, in spite of her exceptional circumstances.

"I can't remember exactly," Sally replied, "sometime in the 70s …".

"You mentioned a boy called Peter?"

"Yes, there was a Peter who lived with us. The home was run by two nursing sisters. Sister Edenborough and Sister Butler. Sister Edenborough adopted Peter. He was a builder and rebuilt St Christopher's after a fire burnt it down."

"That's him! That must be her brother Peter!" I said triumphantly. "She has often talked about him!" I added, without thinking through the implications.

"Definitely! The three of us were brought up as brothers and sisters. What has she said about me?"

It was a fair question, but one which was impossible to answer without hurting her feelings. As far as I was aware the only sister Michele had ever spoken about was me. I dodged the question, telling her instead of how clearly Sharon remembered her childhood trips to Hinton Martell and how fondly she had spoken of Sally.

"I remember Sharon! She was the oldest I think? Michele had three girls and she used to bring them down to Hinton Martell when they were young. Sometimes they came for the day, other times they stayed over."

"When would that have been?" I asked, hopeful that, with Sally's help, I might be able to piece together a rough timeline for Michele's life after she left Guernsey. But the emotion was tiring us both and she was struggling to pinpoint exact dates.

"I'll ask Peter," she said, annoyed with herself that she couldn't remember, "he has a better memory than me. I've often thought about her over the years, you know, and wondered how she is. I named my eldest daughter Michele after her, spelt the same way, with just one l."

I had so many questions I wanted to ask Sally it was difficult to know where to start. But this call was as important to her as it was to me, it would be wrong to bombard her with them all in one go. She clearly loved to reminisce about her upbringing and she had, in me, the perfect audience. But she also had questions of her own. She needed to know what had happened to her best friend after they had lost touch. It was only fair to take turns to share what we knew. So I gave her the space to ask her own questions and answered them as best I could.

"I've remembered the last time I saw her!" she said suddenly, grateful for the information I had given and wanting to reciprocate. "There was an incident in the village, a really unpleasant incident …"

"Oh? What happened?"

"Michele brought the girls down to Hinton Martell one Sunday for lunch. Whilst we were eating we got word that a young man in the village had died suddenly. I rushed to see if I could help and when I got back to St Christopher's they'd gone. I've not seen her since."

"How awful! I don't suppose you've remembered roughly when that might have been?"

"Sometime in the early 1970s, I think? I'll speak to Pete and get back to you tomorrow evening if that's okay? I'm sure he will know. I can't think straight at the moment."

"Of course. Thanks so much, Sally. I'll give Sharon a ring and let her know we've spoken."

As I put the phone down I reflected on our conversation. I had been deeply touched by the affection that Sally had expressed for Michele and the warm way she had spoken about their upbringing. Peter, too, had been a key figure in both of their lives, and Sally and he had always remained close. The three of them had been raised as siblings. It seemed to me the least I could do would be to try to put them back in touch.

I phoned Sharon, who was excited to hear that I had made contact with Sally. Her own memories of their family visits to Hinton Martell were hazy, so the detail that Sally had provided was important to her. We talked through what I might ask Sally in the next call and we both agreed that it would be wonderful if we could put Sally and Michele back in contact with each other.

As I sat down to call Sally the following evening, I had a list of questions and a pen and notepad at the ready. She answered immediately, full of excitement to hear from me again and with, no doubt, a list of her own. We exchanged a few pleasantries and reassured each other of our mutual joy to be in contact; I had been so excited that I had struggled to sleep the previous night; so had she. And then I launched into the first item on my list.

"I spoke to Sharon last night," I began, sensing that the question I was about to ask might have more credibility if it came from her. "She was thrilled we had spoken! But she's still a bit confused! She always thought that Michele was brought up in Guernsey because she talked so much about it. So we were wondering if Michele might have been sent to Guernsey on holiday perhaps, when she was living in the home?"

Sally paused, respectfully, to consider the question. "No. I'm pretty sure she wasn't. We were lucky because we were all sent off somewhere each summer for a holiday, but Michele went to the Isle of Wight I think, or possibly London? The only time I remember her going to Guernsey was when she left St Christopher's and went to work for your mum in her guest-house."

"Would you remember my mum ever visiting her at St Christopher's?" I asked, hopefully.

"She only came once!" she said somewhat abruptly and with a subtle change to her tone that unsettled me. "It was May 1962. We all had German measles at the time so Michele and I were at home together. Michele was in a terrible state after your mum left, she wouldn't get out of bed for days. No one could do anything with her. That's when they sent her to Guernsey …" She stopped herself, sensing she might be going too far, and softened her tone before continuing, "I know this must be hard for you to hear because you obviously love your mum. But I suppose I have always resented her because she took Michele away from us."

I hardly dared ask for more, but I needed to know, and it seemed like she might be ready to tell me. "Have you any idea what happened to Michele after that?"

"She went completely off the rails when she got to Guernsey. I came to look for her you know? To bring her back. I got off the boat and marched straight up the hill to your house. I was very rude to your mother, she had no idea where Michele was. I eventually found her, two days later, and in a bad way …" She stopped again, concerned that this might be too much. "I don't want to upset you Jag?"

"I'm okay Sally. Please go on."

"I didn't know what to do with her, so I brought her back to St Christopher's with me. She worked in the home for a while, but she was determined to move to London. We kept in touch and visited each other from time to time for a few years. But in the late 1970s, I went to live abroad and that's when we finally lost contact."

Sally had been so helpful, it was time that I offered her something in return.

"I was wondering whether you might like me to put you back in touch with her?" I asked quietly.

"I would love that," she whispered.

Choosing my words carefully, I called Michele to tell her that I had just spoken to her oldest friend. She did an impressive job of steadying her voice, but I could sense the anticipation, pleasure and excitement at this unexpected news. With no way of reading her eyes, I judged it best to simply say that Sally would love to speak to her and asked if she would mind if I gave Sally her number. She readily agreed.

"I'll phone her soon," Sally promised, suddenly overcome with emotion, "I just need to compose myself first. It's been a long time ..."

"You'll be fine," I reassured her. "Good luck and let me know how it goes."

"I will. And have a look at your emails. Pete has lent me the journal for St Christopher's, it's the only official document that survived the fire. I thought you might like to see a copy of Michele's entry!"

"Ooooh! Yes please!"

I put the phone down and immediately opened my inbox to find, as promised, an email from Sally. Giddy with anticipation I opened the attachment to reveal a handful of carefully-scripted words; the sum total of my sister's childhood.

And all that remained of child number 403 ...

Le Bargy, Michele Mary. B. 15.1.45. Ad. 28.1.45

Michele Mary! This was the first time I had seen that Michele had been given a middle name ... and it was the same as mine! Amongst the list of her vaccinations, details of her christening and her National Insurance Number was the following statement that supported what Sally had told me the previous evening.

May 1962 German Measles
14th May 1962 Mother Came
2nd June 1962 Discharged to mother
with Mrs Rixon as escort as unfit to remain
at St Christopher's.

Beyond this statement lay the answers to all of my questions, but I knew better than to waste time trying to chase them. It had been written at a time when too much information was considered an unnecessary complication. This was no gateway to the truth, it was a barrier, erected to obscure it. The only thing I knew for certain was that Michele, Sally and Peter had spent seventeen years together at St Christopher's. Happy years according to Sally. It felt good to think that I might have played a small part in bringing them all back together. I wondered how Michele and Sally were getting on catching up on their lost years. What must they both be feeling? I didn't have to wait long to find out.

"It was awful," Sally spluttered, "I can't believe it, Jag."

"You've spoken to her?" I asked, taken aback by her distress, unsure as to what could possibly have gone wrong.

"Yes. I've just phoned her ..." I could sense she was shaking, "I said 'it's Sally' and ..." she broke off.

"And …?" I said gently, trying to help her along; it was terrible to hear her like this.

"… and she said 'Sally who?' And I said 'Sally from St Christopher's' …"

"And …?"

"And she said 'I'm sorry I don't know any Sallys and I've never heard of St Christopher's. I think you must have the wrong number.'"

CHAPTER 7

Brother Peter

I NEVER SPOKE TO Michele about Sally again, but I remained quietly determined to get her to confirm that the Peter from St Christopher's was the brother she had often referred to. A carpenter by trade, he partially fitted her description, and they had certainly been raised together.

When he was twenty-six years old Peter gave up his job, temporarily, to manage the rebuild of St Christopher's which was underinsured when it burned down in 1965. "I haven't got the money but I've got the skill," he told a friend who warned him not to attempt it.

One time, when Michele was visiting Guernsey and seemed relaxed, I decided to try my luck.

"You know you once told me about Mum always taking you back?"

"She did Bubba! She did! She was always taking me back!"

"Well, there was a guy who lived with you called Peter Edenborough, I think?" I watched her face closely for any flicker of recognition, but she remained impassive. "I was wondering if he is the brother Peter that you have told me about?"

"No Bubba!" she said, as if it were a ridiculous suggestion, "not him!"

Had she any recollection of the Peter from St Christopher's? I will never know for sure. She was always the warrior fighting her past, leaving me to trail faithfully behind her, primed and ready to pounce on the titbits of information she occasionally tossed my way. But the conviction with which she denied him ensured that we would continue looking, just in case we found someone that better fit the bill.

One day Charley phoned me, breathless with renewed conviction.

"Peter Le Page!" she said triumphantly. "I'm sure it's him."

"What makes you think that?" I laughed, perhaps a little unkindly considering her enthusiasm.

"I typed everything I knew into Google ... Peter, Builder, Garage, Boats and Guernsey and up he came. Peter Le Page! It must be him!"

I was far from convinced. Le Page is one of the most common surnames in Guernsey and I knew of several Peter Le Pages any one of whom might fit certain of her search criteria. It was absurd that she could hope to find Michele's brother Peter in this way and I set about trying to tell her so. But when Charley is on form she is unstoppable. Before I could comment she had sent me his photograph.

I should have known better than to dismiss her thinking, however unlikely it might seem. Her drive, determination and "thinking outside the box" had, after all, found me. A second photo followed, this time of Michele, but she needn't have taken the trouble as I had already seen the resemblance for myself. My sister and this Peter Le Page did look very much alike. I promised Charley that I'd look locally to try to find out more information about him and immediately contacted my friend, Shona, a former librarian, who had subsequently developed impressive skills in family research.

The common surname and given name meant it took Shona a long time to narrow down the search. Eventually, she established that the most likely 'Peter Le Page' was born in Guernsey in 1946. This was counterintuitive to me as I had always imagined "brother Peter" to be older. However, experience had told me that anything was possible so we agreed that she should try to dig a little deeper.

The discovery that Peter's father owned a building company in Guernsey did little to convince me that she was on the right track, but when Shona mentioned his mother's maiden name, I started to take notice. The name seemed familiar and I felt sure that I had heard my parents refer to her and her family in the past. Further research uncovered the fact that Peter's father had been badly injured during the war, after which he had been stationed some distance from his wife but quite close to Bridgwater. It seemed as though we might be edging closer to finding out the truth. Like Charley, I was beginning to think "outside of the box".

What if Peter's parents had been friends with my parents in Guernsey before the war? Then it was likely that Mum would have kept in contact with them both when they evacuated to the UK. And she would almost certainly have visited his father if she had heard that he had been injured. If a relationship had developed and he was Michele's father, then Peter would be Michele's half-brother but no blood relation to me.

And then Shona discovered that Peter had an older sister who was born in the UK towards the end of the war, just a few months after our Michele. She showed me the record and waited for the coincidence to register. Peter Le Page's sister's name was also Michele, spelt in the same unusual way.

And there was one extra fact that could surely not be down to chance … her middle name was Mary …

CHAPTER 8

Clouds in My Guernsey Sky

PREDICTABLY, THE PETER LE Page enquiry led me down a one-way road towards another dead end. When I eventually managed to track him down he seemed to have no knowledge of Michele and showed no interest in seeing a photo of her despite my mention of their uncanny resemblance.

Meanwhile, our lives plodded along as usual. Rain or shine, Mali and I could still be found on Vazon Beach first thing each morning and most afternoons after school, making the most of whatever the seasons threw at us. For my part, these walks had become times of reflection, of trying to make sense of my ever-changing world. Whilst Mali played joyously around me I would look to the sky for inspiration; a sky that stood witness to the past; a sky that knew all of its secrets. As the clouds, feral and fleeting, danced above me I tried, in vain, to catch their truth. I drew comfort from the thought that the answers were up there somewhere, hidden from view, blown on the wind. It was only when the sky was clear blue and cloudless, revealing everything and nothing, that I was sometimes left feeling a little uneasy.

When dead ends threatened to overwhelm me I took solace in my writing and let it take me to the place where I most wanted to be. The unique story I had uncovered was mine to cherish. I could place it in my book and take refuge in its narrative, surrounded by my parents and my sisters, and anyone else that I wanted to include. At least that's what I hoped. The reality was somewhat different. Writing to satisfy my own needs, and those of my immediate family, was one thing, but if I intended to share the story with a larger audience I would need a completely different skill set. A skill set I didn't possess.

I would have given up had it not been for Pete. The consistency of his support, at every step along the way, had given my journey its foundations. It was his journey, too, and not once did he falter in his commitment to it. The humanity of the story had touched him deeply, he believed it should be shared and he believed in my ability to share it. He encouraged me to join a writing group, a friend of ours was running one, surely that would help? I wasn't so sure but I decided to give it a go. Sure enough, uplifted by the generous spirits of my fellow writers, I began to make modest progress. I emailed some of the instalments to Pauline and she was kind enough to say she enjoyed them, but Michele did not use email and I refrained from telling her of my writing in case it should worry her.

Yet still, the questions remained unanswered. Who was I writing this for? Family and friends? Or a wider audience? And always … would Mum have approved? My memories of her were distant and vague, I had experienced no sense of her in my life for over twenty years. Was she resting in peace or was her spirit in torment? The thoughts gnawed away inside me, sowing the seeds of doubt and thereby winning the argument.

Dad, on the other hand, had never left me. He was my 'shadow person' lurking on the periphery of my life, leaving the occasional, fleeting trace of tobacco in the air, to reassure me of his presence; moving in beside me when I needed guidance, just as he had always done. If what I was doing was wrong he would surely have found a way of letting me know?

Meanwhile, I continued to share my story with a small but ever expanding group of friends.

"Why did your parents never tell you?" people would ask. "Do you think they felt ashamed? Were they worried that you might judge them?" But this was the fundamental question over which I had pondered long and hard, and my thoughts ran deeper than the obvious.

"I sometimes think Mum might have been afraid that she might lose me too," I would offer. Though it was painful to say for, if true, it would show how little she knew me. Eventually I began to wonder if there might be a simpler reason. One that had evolved over time and settled itself, gently, at the core of who we were.

Many times I had thought back to the night in my winter bedroom when Dad told me about Michele. I could still feel the chill in the room and the distress of being told that someone had run away from us. And I could still smell the oil in the wool of Dad's navy blue Guernsey, coarse against my face, as I buried my head in his chest and allowed him to take the blame for misjudging the timing. There would be plenty of other opportunities to tell me he reasoned, as he gathered the blankets around me that night; we surely had many years left. So he wiped away my tears and tucked her story firmly out of reach.

But the years rolled on without Michele and we rolled with them. And, as life swept us along through all its ups and downs, maybe there came a point where he believed that nothing positive could come from resurrecting the past? Sometimes we all leave things too late, we never do find the right time.

There could be no doubt that I had to be told about Michael, however. Tangible evidence existed of his death; Michael had a grave and my parent's intention was to be buried alongside him. It was their duty to tell me because, sooner or later, I was bound to find out.

I am sitting between them on the sofa, in tune with my needs, hostile to theirs. I am fourteen years old and I love Romo, it is the only home I have ever known, and I hate them for insisting that we move. Within me, the argument brews, eagerly awaiting another escape. But they have given up trying to persuade me to consider their needs as well as my own. Today there is a different tension in the air, they have sat me down to tell me something, but I'm not sure they know how to begin.

"Mum and I think you are old enough for us to share something with you, darling ..." Dad starts carefully, aware that I am no longer the little girl that adored him unconditionally, wary as to how the teenage me might react. I remain silent, sullenly determined not to make it easy for him. He flashes a look at Mum, is this really the right time? But she is tired of trying to accommodate me, of trying to reason with the unreasonable. Uncharacteristically, she takes control.

"Before the war, Dad and I had a baby," she says looking directly at me to confirm I am listening. "We called him Michael. We were thrilled because we always wanted a large family. This little boy was our start. But ..." with the briefest of pauses, she heightens the impact "... Michael had a twisted bowel and he died when he was six weeks old. We haven't told you before because we didn't want to upset you. But we thought it was time you should know." Her tone, though matter-of-fact, is laced with weariness; the weariness of a woman battling her own maternal needs.

Dad says nothing. I stare at them, the move long forgotten, eyes bathed in tears for the brother I have never known. Sad for my parents, sad we lost our dream. I fall into their arms, first Mum then Dad, and in that moment I am their child again. Afterwards, when they turn to each other for comfort, I am left to withdraw, back into my own narrow world.

Suddenly it makes perfect sense. This is what Dad had been trying to tell me all those years ago! In my winter bedroom when I was very young. When I pestered him for a brother or sister and he told me about one that had run away. He should have been honest and told me they had died. It was the idea of somebody not loving us that really upset me.

In an instant I had conflated the story of Michael's death with the story of Michele running away from us. For many years, I assumed that Michael and Michele were the same person and that Dad's explanation, in my winter bedroom, was a clumsy attempt at shielding his young daughter from death. I believed that there was one story rather than two, and in so doing I failed to properly understand either of them.

— — —

SATURDAY 18TH FEBRUARY 2017

I had been retired for seven months and Pete and I had spent six of them travelling around the world, embracing the customs and cultures of the countries we visited, absorbing their sounds and smells and tastes, living every moment. In a foreign country, nothing is certain, nothing can be taken for granted, everything needs to be learnt. Travel had changed me. I was ready to look beyond the certainty of my life in Guernsey, to follow the light that shines beyond the clouds, to try to discover the truth that really lay in front of me.

I'd had plenty of time for reflection over the past few months. Long road trips had freed my mind to wander wherever it chose, digging back into my past as I travelled forwards exploring the world; a past that had been blown apart in recent years and only partially put back together. Different journeys brought new perspectives, wider outlooks and a sharper focus on one crucial fact. My parents had not kept Michele a secret from me. I had been told the truth about her several years before they told me about Michael. She had been their priority. It was simply that his story had made sense to me, whilst hers had not.

Refreshed from the trip, and cautiously optimistic that I was doing the right thing, I determined to finish the book I had started writing many years earlier. I had the outline of a few potential chapters stored away in an old file on my computer, but the prospect of turning them into a book was daunting. It was hard to find inspiration on that grey winter's morning so I lit the fire, settled into a comfortable armchair and put on Mum's engagement ring in the hope that I might find encouragement in the tiny sparkle of diamonds.

As I lifted the lid on my laptop and clicked on the introductory chapter, I felt their spirits flood into the room, not just Dad but Mum, too, together at last, just as I remembered them. They swirled around me, playfully, as I immersed myself in the task of transcribing their lives. For two whole days, they watched over me as I wrote, whilst I embraced each tiny hint of their presence with excitement, considering them signs of approval for the continuation of my work. It felt good to languish in their company, but puzzling too, that Mum, in particular, should have come to me after all these years to claim my attention with such persistence.

Late that Sunday evening, after a fruitful weekend writing, I logged into Facebook and, in their honour, changed my profile cover image to a black and white photo of the two of them, young and in love, laughing on the beach. And, as I washed and got ready for bed, I felt their presence in the bathroom with such intensity that it moved me to speak out loud. To ask them:

"What is it that you want …?"

By the next morning, they had left me, just as suddenly as they had appeared. Gone to comfort someone whose need was greater than mine.

CHAPTER 9

Love You More

MONDAY 20TH FEBRUARY 2017 brought a typical winter's day to the Channel Islands. Mild and dreary the clouds hung low in the sky. From time to time a slight rosy hue, suggestive of a dormant sun waking from hibernation, tried and failed to break the cycle of oppression drummed up by the mist and clouds. Despite the gloom, my spirits were high. I was finally back on track with my writing, and Shona had invited me for coffee. She had a theory regarding 'E Woodward 39383 Sick' which, despite my best efforts to persuade her otherwise, she refused to tell me over the phone.

Shona welcomed me into her apartment with open arms and a tight, brief squeeze of excitement. I could smell the coffee, already made, and as she went to pour it she ordered me to make myself comfortable and take a look at the photos on her laptop. I recognised them immediately as two from a batch I had sent her the previous week, placed side by side on the screen for comparison. To the left was the soldier E Woodward and to the right was Pauline at roughly the same age. I looked up and nodded, there were similarities and we both saw them, but any resemblance was far from conclusive.

"You certainly like to give me a challenge!" she said amiably, passing me a coffee and settling herself down next to me. "Woodward is a very common name in the Somerset and Gloucestershire area! There are loads of E Woodwards ..."

"Oh dear! I'm really sorry. Thanks so much for persevering for me."

"Well, I've done my best and I'm pretty sure I've nailed it!" she beamed; pleased with herself; happy for me.

"Knowing you I'm sure you have!" I replied, respectful that this was her moment, impatient for her to share it.

"So … I'm afraid I could find no military record that precisely matched the inscription on your photograph …" I held my breath, unsure what this might mean but conscious it was the beginning and not the end. "I did find one that came very close though …" she said, taking the laptop from me and pulling up a new screen before handing it back. "I'm pretty certain this must be him."

> Edwin Woodward 39883
> Private in the Gloucestershire Regiment WW1 1914-1918
> Wounded on the 15th September 1940.

I studied the record carefully and it took me a while before I saw it. "Wow! So you think she wrote it wrong? A three instead of an eight?"

"Yes. There are no other records that are even vaguely similar. And it's way too much of a coincidence that a different E Woodward could have an almost identical number."

But I was confused; the soldier in the picture looked far too young to have served in WW1? I was about to protest when I realised she had more to tell me.

"Edwin Woodward 39883 had a son, also called Edwin, born on 5th January 1920. I think this must be a photo of Edwin junior," she said, taking time to present her thinking so that I might properly understand it. "And Edwin junior's mother died when he was eight years old."

"So if this is Edwin junior why would Mum have written his father's details on the photo?" I asked, still confused.

"Well, obviously we can't know for sure, but maybe because, in 1942, his father would have been his next of kin?" She said simply, studying me to check that the implications had sunk in before adding, "and it's feasible his father might have been considered 'sick' as a result of his wounds."

So Mum had a photograph of a young soldier, with details of his next of kin, at a time when she was pregnant. The meaning of this we could certainly surmise but, as Shona was quick to point out, it was all just our best guess.

———

Thoughts, like the mist that refused to relinquish its hold over the day, swirled around me as I drove home from Shona's late that morning. I had sensed that the soldier in the photograph might be Pauline's father, and now Shona and I had reasoned that he probably was. Assuming it to be true could he also be Michele's father? I somehow doubted it. Pauline and I were very much alike, but I could find no resemblance between her and Michele, nor between Michele and the soldier in the photograph. If Edwin Woodward was not her father then who was? It was a subject I knew I could never broach with her, she loved my father as if he were her own and the least I could do was have sufficient generosity of spirit to share him.

I wondered how she was? She'd had a thyroid operation the previous week, routine surgery as I understood it, and she was convalescing at home when I'd spoken to her the previous Friday evening. She had sounded cheerful enough but there was a weariness to her voice that suggested I shouldn't keep her on the phone too long.

"Love you," I told her as we said our goodbyes.

"Love you more …" she countered. And I knew not to argue when there was no hope of winning.

I pondered the best way to include Edwin Woodward in my book and was looking forward to getting home to resume my writing. But first I needed to stop off at the supermarket for a few essentials. I had just switched off the car engine when my thoughts were interrupted by the noise of two text messages arriving in quick succession; both from Charley.

I need a number for you x

It's about nan x

I knew in an instant that the news would not be good, but reason could not caution me to even draw breath. Charley answered straight away with the panicked shock of raw grief.

"She's dead … "

"Nan … "

"She died …"

I had no words. No matter, Charley had plenty and she needed to say them. Terrible, unimaginable words that, when strung together, played like an unrehearsed orchestra scratching out a tune that neither of us wanted to hear. There was no applause at the end, just bewilderment on both sides and the deep, dark silence of denial and despair. And afterwards, as I sat in the supermarket car park and looked all around me, it was still Monday lunchtime and people were getting on with their lives as if nothing had happened. And no tears came because it couldn't be true. I sat as if paralysed, waiting for time to rewind and put our lives back on track, or for Charley to phone back to tell me that Michele was fine and it had all been a terrible mistake. But of course it was true and deep down I knew it.

Charley had cut the call short when officials started to arrive at the house.

How could I hope to deal with a loss so deep, so close, so out of reach? I had no idea.

You cannot take chances in life. I had promised to phone her over the weekend but had left it until Monday. I cried inconsolably then, and later, when the tidal wave of tears had finally subsided, I went home to phone Pauline.

CHAPTER 10

The Story Beneath Our Wings

EXHAUSTED BY LATE AFTERNOON, I took my tears to the beach and watched helplessly as they swam before me, cheered on by the venue, relieved at their release. The gloomy fog that had smothered the entire day was disinterested now, in claiming the evening, and blue slithers of a hopeful sky gently intruded to help brighten the mood. The tide was high, just as she loved it, and the dog splashed happily in the waves, unaware of her loss. Michele loved Mali, and Vazon was her favourite place to walk, so I hoped she might join me. But she had chosen a different path and I was left in pieces to make sense of the day.

To understand her death I would first need to understand her life, but Michele was just as enigmatic in both. She had seemed to be recovering well from her operation and had risen early that morning, to make a coffee and let the dog outside. It was an ordinary start to the week in her home in South East London. Whilst Martin went to the shop to fetch the newspapers, she went back to bed to rest, giving no indication that anything was wrong.

When he returned, half an hour later, with the papers and a bacon sandwich, he found her slumped across the bed, unconscious and barely breathing. His call for help was answered by many, but neither he, nor the paramedics, nor her family or friends had any hope of reviving her. She had embarked upon her final journey, one from which no human effort had the power to reclaim her.

Sorrow engulfed her family, jamming their social media threads with heartbreaking tributes that drew in messages of support from all around them. Though my immediate family and friends were wonderful, I struggled to find a channel to express my own grief. My need was to talk to somebody who would feel her passing as much as I did and not someone who might just feel sorry for me. It had helped to talk to Pauline, though she was as stunned as I was with the news. Michele had been bright and cheerful when she had spoken to her the previous day so, like me, she found her death hard to accept. Suddenly, our whole story had lost its happy ending, and Michele's unexpected passing was an injustice we would find hard to bear. We had been caught off guard and, in that heartbeat, she was gone.

Had I done enough, over the years, to welcome her into my life as the sister she should always have been? I thought of the silver box that I had given her, and the letter inside and hoped that I had left her in no doubt of how much I cared.

August 2010

Dearest Mitch,

I've loved having you to stay, thank you so much for coming. You said to me yesterday that we are very different and we certainly are! I just want you to know that I couldn't wish for a nicer sister, I really mean that, thank you for being you and come again whenever you like, you will always be welcome.

You asked me for your birth certificate. Of course you can have it, with pleasure, but I am anxious about giving it to you as I would never want to hurt you in any way but I think it might upset you. You will see that it doesn't mention our dad on it but I wanted to try to explain to you why it doesn't. I thought that maybe the easiest way was for me to write it down in a letter so that you can read it and re-read it to try to make sense of it all, as I have been doing for the past year.

Mum and Dad married on April 20th 1938 at St John's Church, St. Peter Port, Guernsey. They honeymooned in Cornwall. In January 1940 they had a baby boy, Michael John, who had problems feeding. He underwent surgery for a twisted bowel and died on 13th of March 1940 (Mum was always very superstitious and Dad was particularly superstitious about the number 13).

By then World War II had already started and the Germans were advancing towards the Channel Islands. By the June of 1940 it looked like a German occupation of Guernsey was imminent and the islanders were advised to evacuate to the mainland. All women and children were advised to leave and Mum was asked by her father (our grandfather) to evacuate with her youngest sister Dink. There was a lot of confusion on the island at the time, people didn't know whether to go or stay. In the end Mum and Dink decided to go, Mum was 24 and Dink was 17. Our dad was an essential worker at the power station and so was not allowed to leave with them. He had to stay on the island to provide electricity and was to follow them on a later boat. His intention was to join the army – I have found his application forms. As it happened, Mum and Dink were on one of the last boats to leave the island, a couple of days later the Germans bombed the harbour, lots of innocent people were killed, and the next day the Germans occupied the island. For the next five years, no one was allowed in or out of Guernsey and so Mum and Dad were separated by the war with no communication between them except the very occasional Red Cross letters (you have seen the one that I gave to Sharon). These were heavily censored and only 25 words were permitted. They were few and far between and Mum and Dad often went for months without knowing what the other was doing or whether they were safe.

Dad spoke very often about his experiences during the occupation. He spoke of the Germans, daily life, underground movements etc. Mum never ever spoke of her experiences in the UK. All I ever knew was that she lived with a family in Bridgwater, Somerset, and that she worked in a munitions factory. I never thought to ask questions and I am ashamed that I didn't show any interest.

In November 1942 mum gave birth to a baby girl in a nursing home in Torquay, this baby was then adopted. She is our sister - the one that I'm trying to trace. I know nothing about the relationship that led to this child but I do know that our mum had to go away in secret to have the baby. Even in the bleakest of war times, it would still have been a disgrace, as it was for many women, to have a child outside of marriage.

Meanwhile, Dink was also pregnant. Terry (you met him at our barbecue) was born in January 1943. That must have been very difficult for our mum, to see her sister with a baby when she herself had borne two children neither of whom were with her.

In January 1945 you were born in Bournemouth and were named after Michael, her first-born baby son. I believe that she so longed for you that she simply couldn't give you up for adoption. But the war was coming to an end and, on May 9th 1945, the Allied forces liberated Guernsey and the island was set free. Mum would have to return home soon and at that time, with Guernsey very much under the influence of the Methodist Church, it would have been impossible for her to have returned with you. So she returned to Guernsey alone one day in late July. When she got back she found that our dad's mum and sister were also living in her house. Dad's mum moved out quite quickly but Betty (dad's youngest sister) was in no hurry to move. She remembers mum constantly asking her to move out. Mum told her that this was because she wanted to run the place as a guesthouse, but we now believe that it was more likely because mum wanted to bring you there. Meanwhile, in the autumn of 1945, dad was applying for jobs in England and Australia. I have found several rejection letters from different companies. I believe that they were trying to make a new life for themselves away from Guernsey, with you. But times were hard after the war, jobs were scarce and it just didn't happen for them.

In May 1956 I was born and I guess that complicated things quite a lot for everyone. I remember you living with us when I was very young. I remember we shared a room – the room at the top of the house at the back and I do remember that it was like having a sister, though I never had any idea that we were actually sisters! I thought instead that you had come to work in the guest house for the summer season. I remember upsets with mum, I remember Dad trying to smooth things over. I don't remember you leaving but I do remember one night when I was about eight, maybe nine, I kept questioning Dad as to why I had no brothers or sisters, Dad sat on my bed and told me that actually, I did have one (I can't remember whether it was a brother or sister) but that they were unhappy and that they ran away. I have a feeling, still today, that this person ran to the top of the hill and away through the Canichers, but I got so upset at the thought of someone running away from my parents that Dad backtracked on the story and never mentioned it again. Many years later, when Mum and Dad told me about losing our baby brother Michael, I thought back to that night and imagined that Dad must have been referring to Michael, and that, in a misguided attempt to protect me from death he had told me, instead, that he had run away. I remember wishing that dad had told me that he had died rather than that he had run away as it was the running away that had so upset me.

Then, in June last year, I had an email from someone called Charley Miller and suddenly my whole world changed! For me, it has changed for the better. I had always wanted a sister and now I have the best one possible! But the story is incomplete, lots of questions remain unanswered and maybe always will. Perhaps one day you will tell me your story, I long to hear it, but I know the past holds painful memories for you and maybe for you it's better that we just continue with what we have. You can trust that I would always respect that. I hope that what I have written here doesn't upset you, most of it is fact but some of it is based on my own thoughts. I have been researching the story for the past 12 months. It's a tragic wartime story but one that at least has a happy ending with us getting to know each other.

So, Mitch, safe journey home and, as they say in Guernsey, ... "à la perchoine" ... "till we meet again" ... I can't wait.

Love always,

Your sister,

Jag XXX

CHAPTER 11

A la Perchoine

THE SUDDEN NATURE OF Michele's passing meant a considerable delay to the funeral, and it wasn't until mid-March that Pete and I travelled to London to pay our final respects. On arriving in South East London, Charley took me straight to the chapel of rest, and, though I had prepared myself carefully for what I might find there, Michele's form seemed strange and distant and I knew that she had long since left us. Around her neck, she wore a silver necklace with the inscription 'A la Perchoine' (til we meet again) in Guernsey French. It was my first ever Christmas present to her and she had worn it ever since.

Anneka was struggling with the early stages of pregnancy so did not travel with us, but Charlie came up from Brighton that evening. I had never been able to utter a bad word about him to Michele, she simply wouldn't hear of it. To her, he was always her 'Charlie Boy', and even my vaguest observation about the untidiness of his room, or his aversion to homework, would elicit a severe scolding. Such unconditional love and support were special to him and he had loved her dearly for it.

We stayed the night with Charley, on a boat in Greenland Dock which, coincidentally, was called "Roma." And early the next morning we all gathered at Michele's house to await the cortege. In the years that I had known her, Michele had never invited me there, and I felt a little ill at ease at first, as if I were an intruder in my sister's home. The place was warm and full of love and I could see no reason why she wouldn't have wanted me there, but we are all held hostage by false perceptions at times.

The walkways outside Michele's house were flanked with flowers, and a steady stream of mothers, taking their children to the nearby school, paused to admire their beauty and nod to us as a mark of respect. People had assembled outside their houses ready to wave her on her way, and the mood around the square was quietly expectant; until the cortege arrived and its reality chilled us.

The taxis lined up behind the hearse, their doors opened in readiness to receive us but, with rehearsed order forgotten, we fumbled our ways into the first available seats. As we settled ourselves down into the plush interior of the limousines the funeral attendants swept the floral tributes up onto the roofs above us. Blankets of perfume and colour to give us comfort and shelter as we drove down the streets of her life. Every so often the cortege drew to a halt to allow the funeral director time to pick a flower from one of the roofs and place it on the doorstep of the home of an elderly person. Michele had been their carer, but more than that, she was also their friend. Some waved from windows and others from pavements as her community said goodbye to one of its own.

We arrived to a crowd gathered outside the crematorium and I greeted Sally with a warm hug. Stood next to Sally was Pauline and next to her Ken, they had risen early that morning to make the long journey down. I hugged them too, grateful for the support, and the show of solidarity for our sister.

And then Michele's four grandsons, along with her Charlie Boy, raised the coffin high onto their shoulders to carry it with dignity towards her final stand. As the enormity of the moment slowed time to a stop, I turned to embrace Pauline. Overcome with emotion I looked to her for comfort, and we clutched each other tightly as we followed our sister into the crematorium. The three of us together for the very first and the very last time.

We would love her and we would leave her, and afterwards, we would pick up the pieces of our new lives without her. Just as our mother had done 77 years ago to the day when she and my father had said their final goodbyes to our baby brother Michael.

EPILOGUE

Jillian

WHAT A STRANGE PLATFORM time is on which to play out our lives, always driving us forwards, never allowing us to rest. If only I could pause it, just for a moment, to grab hold of my bearings and make sense of the facts that have rewritten my life.

The unanswered questions, and the avenues I have yet to explore, mean the journey continues, chivvied along by the ebb and flow of clues that continue, just occasionally, to be washed up on my shore.

SEPTEMBER 2019

I spotted her in the corner of the restaurant just as we were about to leave. She was sitting with her sister, talking over coffee; they had always been close. I couldn't remember the last time I had seen her, ten years ago maybe? We had been inseparable in our final year at primary school, but the eleven plus had sent us to different schools, and I had seen her just a handful of times since. The hour was late and I was tired but something drew me to her.

"Hi, Jill! Long time no see ... how are you?"

She looked up in surprise. "Jackie! I'm fine thanks. How about you? It's great to see you!"

I introduced Pete, we exchanged a few pleasantries and then, on an impulse, I asked her if she minded if we joined them.

Pete flashed me a look of disbelief. I had barely been awake a few minutes earlier and now I was suggesting prolonging the evening? As we pulled up a couple of chairs I also wondered why I had suggested it.

"I just thought I'd tell you some news that I found out a few years ago that's been quite amazing for me," I started. I had no intention of going into detail, I just wanted to let her know that I now had two sisters and how they had changed my life for the better.

"Sounds exciting!" she said drawing her chair in and leaning over the table towards me. "Tell me!"

"Well! Remember when we were in the fourth year at Amherst and you used to come to my house to play every Saturday?" She nodded. "Remember I was an only child …?"

I thought of our friendship, now a distant memory, yet perfectly preserved in its own tiny bubble of time; untouched by the intervening five decades of our lives. Perhaps I believed that, with her, I could go back to that bubble; back to live at Romo, back to what life was like a few years after Michele left us?

She listened politely as I told her how I had discovered two sisters, following the narrative carefully and smiling when appropriate. But there was an air of neutrality about her that I couldn't quite read. Perhaps she found it strange that, after all these years, I was opening up to her? I kept to my script, and when I had finished I fully expected her to say, "how lovely for you," after which we might all gather our things and go.

Instead, she leaned in closer and said in a hushed voice. "You never knew you had a sister?"

"No! I had no idea."

She looked startled, as if she were suddenly caught centre stage and had forgotten her lines.

"Jill? What is it?"

"Well …" she started "… I feel awful about this … but honestly … I had no idea that you didn't know … I don't want to upset you …"

"Jill please! Just tell me." This was not going at all as I had expected.

"Well … the thing is … I knew you had a sister!"

"You knew I had a sister?!" Even the repeat of her statement could not convince me. How could she possibly know?

"Yes," she answered simply, relieved that she had finally found the words, "I always knew."

"But how did you know?"

"Your mum told me."

I pulled myself out of the intensity of the moment, sat back in my chair and stared at her in disbelief. She pulled back too, unsure as to what I might do next, waiting, and wishing maybe, that fate hadn't placed us together in this particular moment. But I couldn't let it rest, however awkward it was making her feel.

"But why would my mum tell you that?"

"Because there was a photo of a young girl on the TV in your lounge and one day I asked your mum who she was. She told me she was your sister."

I still couldn't quite believe what she was saying, but she was gaining the courage to continue, to try to find the proof that might finally convince me.

"You also had a brother, didn't you? Who died when he was a baby? There was a photo of him too, I think his name was Michael?"

I nodded, but no words came.

"I'm so sorry, Jackie, I thought you knew all of this."

But I was no longer listening …

From my attic bedroom, I hear voices in the hallway below. Someone has arrived, I am sure it is her; she comes every Saturday at about this time, her dad brings her.

I wait, impatiently, for her to come up to see me. I have a new game, I'm eager to play.

Five minutes pass and still she hasn't come. But I know where she is, this has happened before. I hurry down the stairs and find her, comfortably at home, sitting on the sofa in the lounge, reading a book. Why is she sitting reading instead of coming upstairs?

My mother enters the room, intercepting my frustrations in the nick of time. She knows I am upset. Silently I implore her to tell my friend to come. But Mum is fond of Jill, and today she is on the side of the reader lost perhaps, like her, in someone else's story.

"You go back upstairs, darling," she says. "I'm sure Jill will be up as soon as she has finished her chapter." Jill smiles up at her gratefully and resumes her reading.

I climb the stairs back to my attic bedroom, leaving the two of them in the lounge. There is no point arguing. They have a liking between them, a genuine warmth. Perhaps Mum will coax Jill away from her book and persuade her to come up to play with me.

Or perhaps today will be the day that she speaks the truth out loud, simply to remember who she is.

EXHIBIT A

Official Instructions to Evacuees

CHILDREN SHOULD TAKE WITH them on evacuation the following articles: Gas masks, Two ration books (current and new one).

Besides the clothes which the child will be wearing, which should include an overcoat or mackintosh, a complete change of clothing should be carried. The following is suggested:

GIRLS	BOYS
One vest or combination	One vest
One pair of knickers	One shirt with collar
One bodice	One pair of pants
One petticoat	One pullover or jersey
Two pairs of stockings	One pair of knickers
Handkerchiefs	Handkerchiefs
Slip and blouse	Two pairs of socks or stockings
Cardigan	

Additional for all: Night attire, comb, towel, soap, face-cloth, tooth-brush and, if possible, boots and shoes and plimsolls.

The Rations: Rations for the journey: Sandwiches (egg or cheese); Packets of nuts and seedless raisins; Dry biscuits (with little packets of cheese); Barley sugar (rather than chocolate); Apple; Orange.

Source: *The Star*, Guernsey, 19 June 1940.

EXHIBIT B

The Red Cross Civilian Postal Message Scheme

ONE OF THE FIRST actions of the German forces when they arrived in the Channel Islands in June 1940, was to cut all telephone and telegraph connections between the islands and England. Mailships had already ceased their regular service with the islands.

This left islanders starved of news with the outside world, and their family members in the armed forces, or evacuated in England, were similarly deprived of news of what was happening in the islands.

Unlike prisoners-of-war, there were no international conventions regarding communications with civilians in occupied territories – but in the early years of the war, the International Red Cross managed to negotiate an agreement between belligerents and the Red Cross Civilian Postal Message Scheme was born. By the end of 1940, it was fully established and the first messages started arriving in Guernsey in January 1941.

This service allowed messages of no more than twenty-five words to be sent to family members using a special form and a reply of the same length to be sent in return. Each household was restricted to one message per month.

Messages were strictly limited to personal information only, and were scrutinised by a German censor in Guernsey to weed out any forms attempting to divulge sensitive information.

Messages from family members in England were delivered to the Red Cross bureau in Guernsey via neutral Switzerland, which had maintained a postal service with both England

and Germany. In order to reach Switzerland, messages from Guernsey had to travel first via Paris and Berlin before transmission to the International Red Cross Headquarters. From there they were passed to the Royal Mail for delivery.

This did not make for an efficient service – it typically took more than six months from sending a message to receiving a reply. Replies to the first messages sent from Guernsey in July 1941 started arriving in the island in January/ February 1942.

Between January 1941 and June 1944, approximately 250,000 incoming messages were received and replied to – and a similar number were sent from the island during the same period.

After the liberation of Normandy in June 1944, the regular postal service between the islands and Germany was severed and, apart from a small number of messages carried by the Red Cross ship, SS Vega, there was no service at all.

The two thousand Channel Islanders who were deported to prison camps in Germany in 1942-43, such as Biberach, had access to the service for prisoners-of-war – which allowed longer letters, photographs and even parcels to be sent from England to the internees. Communications between internees and the Channel Islands could use the regular mail service, which continued to operate between the islands and Germany, as well as other German-occupied territories in Europe until D-Day.

For more details of the Red Cross Message Scheme in Guernsey, see *Waists Getting Waspish* by Leopold Mayr (CISS, 2017). For mail between the Channel Islands and the internees in German prison camps, see *Islanders Deported (Part 2)* by Roger E Harris (CISS, 1983).

EXHIBIT C

Advice to Guernsey Refugees

No Return for Some Considerable Time

THE FOLLOWING IS THE text of a circular issued by Mr M E Weatherall, hon secretary of the Channel Islands Refugee Committee:-

My committee have received many enquiries as to how, on the reoccupation of the Channel Islands by the British:-

(a)   refugees now in Great Britain may at once return to their homes, and

(b)   how persons in the Islands may at once come to the United Kingdom.

While nothing can be said as to what may be expected to happen on the reoccupation of the Channel Islands, since no one knows under what conditions that reoccupation will take place, and what the state of the Islands will be, it is clear that under the most favourable conditions:-

For a considerable time no one will be able to go to the islands whose services there are not urgently required for work connected with the war efforts, and

only in the most exceptional cases will anyone be allowed to leave the Islands.

The demands upon our shipping will remain tremendous, and there is no likelihood that an early date shipping will be available to establish either a passenger service between the Islands and the mainland, or to carry to the Islands such extra supplies as an addition to their present population would entail.

Exhibit C

It must always be remembered that there is a possibility that much will have to be done in the Islands before they are really habitable by their present inhabitants, and still more before they can receive back those refugees now in the United Kingdom

The widest publicity will be given to all news from the Islands, and to news affecting refugees over here. Those whose services will be required will be called upon.

Source: *The Channel Islands Monthly Review,* Journal of Channel Island Refugees in Great Britain, June 1944

EXHIBIT D

Central Advisory Committee Formed

Unity of Purpose the Aim

AT A MEETING IN London on April 13th, 1945, attended by representative people from the Channel Islands, it was decided to set up a committee to be known as the "Central Advisory Committee for Channel Island Affairs." This committee, which is composed chiefly of people with interest to return to the Channel Islands as soon as possible, will study the problems which will exist in the islands when they are cleared of the Germans.

To all connected with the various Channel Island Societies in the United Kingdom it is clear that widespread anxiety exists among the refugees, both as to how questions of policy will be dealt with, and about their own personal problems. There is among them a very general desire to have somebody to which to turn for information and advice. So far as personal questions are concerned they have hitherto looked to the Channel Islands Refugee Committee, which has done what is necessary. The charter of this body limits its scope, however, and its purpose will be fulfilled as soon as the return to the Islands is possible. For the various problems which will then face the islanders there is no organization to which they can look for guidance. These problems will be the concern, not only of the returned refugees, but equally of their kinsmen who remained in the Islands.

Five years of separation and widely different living conditions cannot fail to give each of the two groups a different outlook; nor is this the only difficulty, for the stress and strain of the Occupation is said to have brought about differences among those who remained, two of the principal causes being the attitude adopted towards the Occupying Power and the Black Market.

Thus it may be anticipated that at least three groups will be concerned in building the future for the prosperity and happiness of the Islands. Unless a large measure of "give and take" can be achieved among all islanders and unless each group can bring itself to allow that the others also have a point of view, and unless all are prepared to find common ground for their mutual benefit, rehabilitation may be a bitter and prolonged process.

Unity of aim for the common good thus becomes the primary necessity for all, and to ensure this some machinery is necessary. The need for unity does seem to have been recognized by the refugees and several honest attempts to achieve this have been made by different groups; unfortunately, these, for various reasons, have not so far appealed to all, and the essential unity of purpose remains unattained. It is in the hope of providing the coordinating body now so urgently needed that the new committee has been formed.

Time is getting short, yet if in the limited period at their disposal Channel Islanders in this country can make of this committee an organisation in which all can combine, and through which their diverse views can be expressed, half the battle will be won. It would then remain for the new body to persuade those in the Islands to join with them in making their organisation a clearing house for their affairs, and to give it the power truly to represent the considered opinions of all …

Source: *The Channel Islands Monthly Review*, May 1945

EXHIBIT E

Channel Islands Refugees Committee

June 11, 1945

THE GOVERNMENT HAVE BEEN considering as a matter of urgency, with the commander of the military forces and with representatives of the States in the Channel Islands, plans for the repatriation of persons to the Channel Islands.

The immediate return to the islands of large numbers of persons would create very serious problems of accommodation and unemployment, and at the outset provision can be made for the return of only a few hundred persons per week. Later the rate will increase as employment and accommodation become available.

The island authorities will be responsible for allotting priorities, and persons who will be selected for early return will be Channel Islanders for whom there is immediate employment in the islands and those who have homes to go to and for whom reabsorption would not create local problems. There will be no question of holidaymakers visiting the island this year. Returning residents who will be allowed to take with them a reasonable amount of luggage but household goods will have to be sent by cargo steamer and arrangements for this purpose are at present being made.

All residents of Jersey, Guernsey, or Sark wishing to return should apply by post and not in person, to the passport office, Channel Islands section, Dartmouth Street, London, S.W.1, for the forms of application. They will be told how to proceed and will be notified when their return to the Channel Islands has been authorised. It is particularly requested that an application for return to the islands should not be made unless the applicant is prepared to travel at short notice.

In addition to those returning to their homes in this way arrangements will be made for priority passages for persons travelling on urgent compassionate grounds, for example to visit near relatives who are critically ill. The public are requested to refrain from applying for travel on compassionate grounds unless there is real necessity for immediate travel.

The return of the population of Alderney is being considered separately, and these arrangements do not apply to Alderney.

The above information has been given to us for circulation by the Home Office.

M.E.WEATHERALL, Hon. Director.

ACKNOWLEDGEMENTS

A GREAT MANY PEOPLE have shared in this journey with me, some have been on board for the whole trip and others have dipped in and out as I've needed them, keeping me on the straight and narrow, cheering me on from the sidelines. I am eternally grateful for this wealth of support; my life is blessed because of you all.

To my husband, Peter. There would be no book without you. I see how our story touches you, as deeply as it touches me, and without your compassion and empathy I would never have had the motivation to put pen to paper. Your unwavering confidence in my ability to write, and your insistence that opening the story up to a wider audience was the right thing to do, was the fuel that kept me going during all the times I felt I was running on empty. Thank you for being there every step of the way. I love you.

To my wonderful Guernsey family. Thank you for being travelling companions on this rocky road through life. Through all our ups and downs it is your love and support that gives my life its purpose.

To my ray of sunshine, Anneka, you are a wonderful mum to our little treasure. Your love of life is inspirational and infectious. Thank you for sharing it with me.

To Charlie, our square peg in the round hole of life. Through you I have come to see the world from a different perspective. Thank you for being you and for the wonderful music that provides the backdrop to our lives still.

To James and Edward, thank you for your acceptance and your love; the strength and support that you give me means the world to me.

And to Tara, Pete and Sharon, thank you for your good humour, for always mucking in and for the balance you bring to our brood.

To Tayla, Robyn, Jess, Harry, George and Hendrick. You are our future. Thank you for your sense of fun; for keeping me young whilst wearing me out; and thank you especially for your unconditional love.

To dear Auntie Betty, at 100 years old you are a real treasure. Thank you for the kindness you have always shown me and thank you for sharing all the fascinating stories of your past so freely.

To Pauline, my big sister, friend and confidant, thank you from the bottom of my heart for saying yes when it might have seemed simpler to have said no. Thank you for opening your arms to embrace me as we walked together towards a future I never thought possible and thank you for sticking with it for the duration.

And to Ken and Martin, love and thanks to you both for your endless support and encouragement.

To my new extended families, thank you for becoming a part of my life and for enriching it beyond measure. Special thanks to Sharon and Charley, without whom I would have no story. Thank you for your tenacity, for digging deep, for never giving up and for caring about it all as much as I do. Special thanks to Emma, too, for your generosity of spirit and for embracing your Nana with such ease.

To the very many people in my life that I have the privilege of calling friends, your love and support means everything to me. Thanks to my walking buddies, my dance buddies, my swim buddies, my old school friends and special thanks to my uni buddies for allowing me to use a small part of you. Thank you for the support and encouragement you have shown me, for the teas, the coffees, the wine. I take none of it for granted, thank you for always being there, for caring, for your love.

To Sally, thank you for all the hours you spent talking to me about the past. The memories you shared helped me build a picture of my sister as she was growing up, and for me that was priceless. I am sad and sorry that my gain seemed to be at your loss.

To Pippa and the members of our little group of generously spirited writers with whom I took my first tentative writing steps. Thank you for the interest you showed in my story and the encouragement you gave me to write it. You sowed the seeds of confidence that gave me the courage to continue.

To Patricia, thank you for your kindness and your common sense approach in guiding me through the process of reaching out to my adopted sister. And to my research friend, thanks for all your efforts on my behalf and your determination to track down the missing pieces of the puzzle.

Thanks to the wonderfully patient Steve, at Ormer Publishing, for helping me to publish. It is a story owned by so many and it felt right to place it in your kind, safe hands. Thanks to the incredibly talented artist, James Colmer, for the beautifully painted cover. And special thanks to Jane for the thankless task of proof reading and correcting my many errors, and to all those who made it slightly easier for her by trudging through the earlier versions of the book and giving me feedback; Shona, Sheila, Sara, Jenny, Mandy, Lotta and Candy.

And to those for whom the journey has now ended, thank you for the love and the laughter that you have left in my heart.

To Mitch, whom I have loved and lost twice. As our dad used to say, "good things come to those that wait". Thank you for trusting me with our sisterhood, for loving and caring about me and for never holding me to account for the past.

Love you more.

To my beautiful cousin who danced and sang, laughed and cried with me through all the highs and lows of our lives. Rest easy my darling and thank you for everything.

To my dad, who walks beside me still, gently, imperceptibly guiding my path. Thank you for your love and your compassion. You remain now, as always, the hero of the story, the centre of my world.

And to my mum, a closed woman with an open heart, I love you more than ever. Thank you for always putting my needs before your own and for not burdening me with the weight of your despair. Life has eventually brought you the chance, through me, to reach back to your lost daughters. I hope this brings you peace.

And finally thanks to you, the reader, for taking the time to share in this journey with me.

Jag Sherbourne
Guernsey, January 2023

ABOUT THE AUTHOR

JAG SHERBOURNE is a retired maths teacher who wrote this heart-warming memoir after an email from a stranger raised questions about her family's past.

Jag lives with her husband, Peter, in a cottage on the west coast of Guernsey. They share a passion for education, adventure and a deep love for their large family. When not travelling, you will find Jag on the dance floor, in the sea or walking with friends.